LET'S ELIMINATE YOUR LIMITS

How to FINALLY Achieve the Goals You Set

PERSONAL JOURNAL

ഏഏഏ

❦❦❦

Property of:

_____

A simple method for finally achieving the goals you set, no matter what they are or how many times you've tried and failed.

❧❧❧

SIMPLICITY + CONSISTENCY

That's the masterstroke of this process.

To know where you're going.

To feel where you're going.

To constantly imagine where you're going.

But to get there by doing simple things consistently.

For five years now, we've been doing exactly that.

45-60 minutes every day spent on setting our minds, our hearts, our thoughts, our actions, and our behaviors in alignment with our goals.

And it works.

Because SIMPLICITY + CONSISTENCY are the two variables that make ANYTHING possible.

The body you want.

The money you want.

The business you want.

The relationship you want.

The life you want.

It's not about trying to hit a home run every time you're at bat.

Yes. Home runs are sexy.

But when you concentrate on hitting singles every single day, you win the game.

And you don't have to spend your life in the dramatics of gearing up to hopefully spank that one fluky pitch into the bleachers.

A failure-proof method that allows you to set any goal you want and actually achieve it... in less time than you think.

✧✧✧

This process is all about learning to OWN YOUR PERSPECTIVE.

Reality is an illusion.

And if you're currently stuck in the mire of troubled health, finances, fitness levels, or relationships, you may just hate us for saying that.

But let us be VERY clear on this.

These words are coming from a man who spent twelve years clinically depressed.

Who tried to end his own life four times and thought about it virtually every day.

A woman who spent nearly two decades in the quiet torment of people pleasing.

Who was near bankruptcy for most of those two decades.

Until we created and started using this exact process (that we still use to this day).

What we've learned through it all has changed our lives.

Truth is, there is no reality.

There is the reality you choose to see.

There is no label of what you are.

There is the label of what you choose to permit yourself to become.

And that is ALL a choice.

More than you realize.

We stopped seeing the reality we had been handed and started seeing the reality we wanted.

Period.

A literal "plug and play" method that doesn't involve hours of learning or figuring things out... all so you can start creating the changes you want in life as early as today.

࿇࿇࿇

We were able to do that because of these four daily habits.

➢ We counted our wins rather than getting on ourselves for what we weren't doing enough of.

➢ We reviewed our direction by holding the vision of what we wanted, trusting the process that would get us there, and committing to making it happen.

➢ We learned our language and aligned our self-talk with what we wanted, instead of what we didn't.

➢ We imagined achieving what we wanted instead of paying more attention to how much work was left to be done to achieve it.

And it all worked.

For us.

For the hundreds of people worldwide we coached.

And now...

...For you.

Let's Eliminate Your Limits, Together.

Brian & Carrie

❧❧❧
Instructions
❧❧❧

The daily workbook has been created for you as a way to implement the methods of this program into your day-to-day practices in order to achieve the goals that you have set.

The workbook is simple in both its instructions and use. However, you have to do the work to make it work.

Be sure to go through the exercises everyday as was to ensure that you are priming yourself for the success that you want.

❧❧❧
Learn Your Language
❧❧❧

Remember that... Learning your language is the daily action of aligning your inner voice with the success of your goals.

How to do this exercise:

➤ Do this exercise once a day in for a duration of about 5 minutes.

➤ Remove yourself of distraction (people, work) that may take you away from being able to focus on listening to your thoughts.

➤ Think about your current goals that you are working towards - do not filter your thoughts or feelings as they come to you.

➤ Write down all the limiting thoughts and feelings that come to you in the journal.

Review Your Direction

Remember that... Reviewing your direction is the daily action of reviewing and reflecting on your goals.

How to do this exercise:

> ➢ Do this exercise for your top 3 goals but go through them one at a time.
>
> ➢ List your current goal in the identified space in your journal.
>
> ➢ After writing it down spend a few moments reflecting on that particular goal and write down the thoughts that come to mind. Remember the intention is to create a positive reflection of the direction you are traveling in.
>
> ➢ Use the question/statements listed below to help you facilitate the process of reviewing your direction
>
>   - Think about where you were when you set this goal and reflect on how far you have come. Find perspective of growth on the small things as well.
>   - What will it feel like for you when you achieve the goal you set?
>   - Why did you set this goal in the first place?
>   - What are you going to do as a celebration of achieving this goal?

Count Your Wins

Remember that... Counting your wins is the daily action of listing the forward progress of your goals.

How to do this exercise:

> ➢ Holding your current goals at the top of your mind reflect on the last 24 hours
>
> ➢ List all the things that you can't think of that you did that moved you closer to achieving your goals

- Hold top of the mind that a 'win' does not have to be a big AHA experience because the little things that add up day by day create the success you are looking for.

- Remember that even on a day that you might not have been ideal in your targets you can find wins

- Use the following as considerations as you are thinking.
  - Wins might be small in size but are significant in the growth process. (ie: if you didn't go to the gym when you really wanted to but didn't beat yourself up with internal language that was limiting)
  - Wins will be dynamic and change from day to day - hold today as your vision not yesterday or tomorrow. (ie: If you had a brilliant week of work but then woke up one day sick and unable to focus perhaps your work day wasn't as effective but a win might be the fact that you actually managed to get everything done even though it was slower than usual you didn't call it quits)

❧❧❧

Imagine Your Outcome

❧❧❧

Remember that... Imagine your outcome is the daily action of imagining yourself having achieved your goals.

How to do this exercise:

- Perform this exercise as a standing appointment with yourself for 10-minutes daily or throughout the day at varying intervals.

- Hold the visual image of you accomplishing your goal(s) in your conscious attention. Create a vision that allows you to 'see' the image of this. (ie: create a 'scene' that encompasses the success of your goals)

- As other thoughts come in and distract you, re-center your focus on the air coming into and out of your nostrils, while gently guiding your conscious attention back to the desired visual image.

- Once you have completed the exercise fill in the journal section associated in order to reflect on the experience.

Today's Date: _____

Learn My Language: What is my language telling me today?

_____

_____

_____

_____

Review My Direction:

Goal #1: _____

What are my reflections about this goal?

_____

_____

_____

_____

Goal #2: _____

What are my reflections about this goal?

_____

_____

_____

_____

Goal #3: _____

What are my reflections about this goal?

_____

_____

_____

_____

Count My Wins:

What did I do today that helped move me closer to achieving my goals? (List everything you can think of.)

_____

_____

_____

_____

_____

_____

_____

My One Thing: Pick one win from above and isolate that as your greatest step towards success.

_____

Imagine Your Outcome.

What time of day did you perform this exercise? _____

Describe how you felt (using 2 words) prior to performing it: _____ & _____

Describe how you felt (using 2 words) after performing it: _____ & _____

List any challenges you had during the exercise:

_____

_____

_____

Describe two positive and memorable moments, thoughts, or feelings you experienced during the exercise:

_____

_____

_____

Hold the Vision. Trust the Process. Commit to Today.

Today's Date: _____

Learn My Language: What is my language telling me today?

_____

_____

_____

_____

Review My Direction:

Goal #1: _____

What are my reflections about this goal?

_____

_____

_____

_____

Goal #2: _____

What are my reflections about this goal?

_____

_____

_____

_____

Goal #3: _____

What are my reflections about this goal?

_____

_____

_____

_____

Count My Wins:

What did I do today that helped move me closer to achieving my goals? (List everything you can think of.)

_____

_____

_____

_____

_____

_____

_____

My One Thing: Pick one win from above and isolate that as your greatest step towards success.

_____

Imagine Your Outcome.

What time of day did you perform this exercise? _____

Describe how you felt (using 2 words) prior to performing it: _____ & _____

Describe how you felt (using 2 words) after performing it: _____ & _____

List any challenges you had during the exercise:

_____

_____

Describe two positive and memorable moments, thoughts, or feelings you experienced during the exercise:

_____

_____

Hold the Vision. Trust the Process. Commit to Today.

Today's Date: _____

Learn My Language: What is my language telling me today?

_____

_____

_____

_____

Review My Direction:

Goal #1: _____

What are my reflections about this goal?

_____

_____

_____

_____

Goal #2: _____

What are my reflections about this goal?

_____

_____

_____

_____

Goal #3: _____

What are my reflections about this goal?

_____

_____

_____

_____

Count My Wins:

What did I do today that helped move me closer to achieving my goals? (List everything you can think of.)

_____

_____

_____

_____

_____

_____

_____

My One Thing: Pick one win from above and isolate that as your greatest step towards success.

_____

Imagine Your Outcome.

What time of day did you perform this exercise? _____

Describe how you felt (using 2 words) prior to performing it: _____ & _____

Describe how you felt (using 2 words) after performing it: _____ & _____

List any challenges you had during the exercise:

_____

_____

Describe two positive and memorable moments, thoughts, or feelings you experienced during the exercise:

_____

_____

_____

Hold the Vision. Trust the Process. Commit to Today.

Today's Date: _____

Learn My Language: What is my language telling me today?

_____

_____

_____

_____

Review My Direction:

Goal #1: _____

What are my reflections about this goal?

_____

_____

_____

_____

Goal #2: _____

What are my reflections about this goal?

_____

_____

_____

_____

Goal #3: _____

What are my reflections about this goal?

_____

_____

_____

_____

Count My Wins:

What did I do today that helped move me closer to achieving my goals? (List everything you can think of.)

_____

_____

_____

_____

_____

_____

_____

_____

My One Thing: Pick one win from above and isolate that as your greatest step towards success.

_____

Imagine Your Outcome.

What time of day did you perform this exercise? _____

Describe how you felt (using 2 words) prior to performing it: _____ & _____

Describe how you felt (using 2 words) after performing it: _____ & _____

List any challenges you had during the exercise:

_____

_____

_____

Describe two positive and memorable moments, thoughts, or feelings you experienced during the exercise:

_____

_____

_____

Hold the Vision. Trust the Process. Commit to Today.

Today's Date: _____

Learn My Language: What is my language telling me today?

_____

_____

_____

_____

Review My Direction:

Goal #1: _____

What are my reflections about this goal?

_____

_____

_____

_____

Goal #2: _____

What are my reflections about this goal?

_____

_____

_____

_____

Goal #3: _____

What are my reflections about this goal?

_____

_____

_____

_____

Count My Wins:

What did I do today that helped move me closer to achieving my goals? (List everything you can think of.)

_____

_____

_____

_____

_____

_____

_____

_____

My One Thing: Pick one win from above and isolate that as your greatest step towards success.

_____

Imagine Your Outcome.

What time of day did you perform this exercise? _____

Describe how you felt (using 2 words) prior to performing it: _____ & _____

Describe how you felt (using 2 words) after performing it: _____ & _____

List any challenges you had during the exercise:

_____

_____

_____

Describe two positive and memorable moments, thoughts, or feelings you experienced during the exercise:

_____

_____

_____

Hold the Vision. Trust the Process. Commit to Today.

Today's Date: _____

Learn My Language: What is my language telling me today?

_____

_____

_____

_____

Review My Direction:

Goal #1: _____

What are my reflections about this goal?

_____

_____

_____

_____

Goal #2: _____

What are my reflections about this goal?

_____

_____

_____

_____

Goal #3: _____

What are my reflections about this goal?

_____

_____

_____

_____

Count My Wins:

What did I do today that helped move me closer to achieving my goals? (List everything you can think of.)

_____

_____

_____

_____

_____

_____

_____

_____

My One Thing: Pick one win from above and isolate that as your greatest step towards success.

_____

Imagine Your Outcome.

What time of day did you perform this exercise? _____

Describe how you felt (using 2 words) prior to performing it: _____ & _____

Describe how you felt (using 2 words) after performing it: _____ & _____

List any challenges you had during the exercise:

_____

_____

_____

Describe two positive and memorable moments, thoughts, or feelings you experienced during the exercise:

_____

_____

_____

Hold the Vision. Trust the Process. Commit to Today.

Today's Date: _____

Learn My Language: What is my language telling me today?

_____

_____

_____

_____

Review My Direction:

Goal #1: _____

What are my reflections about this goal?

_____

_____

_____

_____

Goal #2: _____

What are my reflections about this goal?

_____

_____

_____

_____

Goal #3: _____

What are my reflections about this goal?

_____

_____

_____

_____

Count My Wins:

What did I do today that helped move me closer to achieving my goals? (List everything you can think of.)

_____

_____

_____

_____

_____

_____

_____

_____

My One Thing: Pick one win from above and isolate that as your greatest step towards success.

_____

Imagine Your Outcome.

What time of day did you perform this exercise? _____

Describe how you felt (using 2 words) prior to performing it: _____ & _____

Describe how you felt (using 2 words) after performing it: _____ & _____

List any challenges you had during the exercise:

_____

_____

_____

Describe two positive and memorable moments, thoughts, or feelings you experienced during the exercise:

_____

_____

_____

Hold the Vision. Trust the Process. Commit to Today.

Today's Date: _____

Learn My Language: What is my language telling me today?

_____

_____

_____

_____

Review My Direction:

Goal #1: _____

What are my reflections about this goal?

_____

_____

_____

_____

Goal #2: _____

What are my reflections about this goal?

_____

_____

_____

_____

Goal #3: _____

What are my reflections about this goal?

_____

_____

_____

_____

Count My Wins:

What did I do today that helped move me closer to achieving my goals? (List everything you can think of.)

_____

_____

_____

_____

_____

_____

_____

_____

My One Thing: Pick one win from above and isolate that as your greatest step towards success.

_____

Imagine Your Outcome.

What time of day did you perform this exercise? _____

Describe how you felt (using 2 words) prior to performing it: _____ & _____

Describe how you felt (using 2 words) after performing it: _____ & _____

List any challenges you had during the exercise:

_____

_____

_____

Describe two positive and memorable moments, thoughts, or feelings you experienced during the exercise:

_____

_____

_____

Hold the Vision. Trust the Process. Commit to Today.

BRIAN & CARRIE
LET'S ELIMINATE YOUR LIMITS
WWW.BRIANANDCARRIE.LIVE

Today's Date: _____

Learn My Language: What is my language telling me today?

_____

_____

_____

_____

Review My Direction:

Goal #1: _____

What are my reflections about this goal?

_____

_____

_____

_____

Goal #2: _____

What are my reflections about this goal?

_____

_____

_____

_____

Goal #3: _____

What are my reflections about this goal?

_____

_____

_____

_____

Count My Wins:

What did I do today that helped move me closer to achieving my goals? (List everything you can think of.)

_____

_____

_____

_____

_____

_____

_____

_____

My One Thing: Pick one win from above and isolate that as your greatest step towards success.

_____

Imagine Your Outcome.

What time of day did you perform this exercise? _____

Describe how you felt (using 2 words) prior to performing it: _____ & _____

Describe how you felt (using 2 words) after performing it: _____ & _____

List any challenges you had during the exercise:

_____

_____

_____

Describe two positive and memorable moments, thoughts, or feelings you experienced during the exercise:

_____

_____

_____

Hold the Vision. Trust the Process. Commit to Today.

BRIAN & CARRIE
LET'S ELIMINATE YOUR LIMITS
WWW.BRIANANDCARRIE.LIVE

Today's Date: _____

Learn My Language: What is my language telling me today?

_____

_____

_____

_____

Review My Direction:

Goal #1: _____

What are my reflections about this goal?

_____

_____

_____

_____

Goal #2: _____

What are my reflections about this goal?

_____

_____

_____

_____

Goal #3: _____

What are my reflections about this goal?

_____

_____

_____

_____

Count My Wins:

What did I do today that helped move me closer to achieving my goals? (List everything you can think of.)

_____

_____

_____

_____

_____

_____

_____

_____

My One Thing: Pick one win from above and isolate that as your greatest step towards success.

_____

Imagine Your Outcome.

What time of day did you perform this exercise? _____

Describe how you felt (using 2 words) prior to performing it: _____ & _____

Describe how you felt (using 2 words) after performing it: _____ & _____

List any challenges you had during the exercise:

_____

_____

_____

Describe two positive and memorable moments, thoughts, or feelings you experienced during the exercise:

_____

_____

_____

Hold the Vision. Trust the Process. Commit to Today.

Today's Date: _____

Learn My Language: What is my language telling me today?

_____

_____

_____

_____

Review My Direction:

Goal #1: _____

What are my reflections about this goal?

_____

_____

_____

_____

Goal #2: _____

What are my reflections about this goal?

_____

_____

_____

_____

Goal #3: _____

What are my reflections about this goal?

_____

_____

_____

_____

Count My Wins:

What did I do today that helped move me closer to achieving my goals? (List everything you can think of.)

_____

_____

_____

_____

_____

_____

_____

_____

My One Thing: Pick one win from above and isolate that as your greatest step towards success.

_____

Imagine Your Outcome.

What time of day did you perform this exercise? _____

Describe how you felt (using 2 words) prior to performing it: _____ & _____

Describe how you felt (using 2 words) after performing it: _____ & _____

List any challenges you had during the exercise:

_____

_____

_____

Describe two positive and memorable moments, thoughts, or feelings you experienced during the exercise:

_____

_____

_____

Hold the Vision. Trust the Process. Commit to Today.

Today's Date: _____

Learn My Language: What is my language telling me today?

_____

_____

_____

_____

Review My Direction:

Goal #1: _____

What are my reflections about this goal?

_____

_____

_____

_____

Goal #2: _____

What are my reflections about this goal?

_____

_____

_____

_____

Goal #3: _____

What are my reflections about this goal?

_____

_____

_____

_____

Count My Wins:

What did I do today that helped move me closer to achieving my goals? (List everything you can think of.)

_____

_____

_____

_____

_____

_____

_____

My One Thing: Pick one win from above and isolate that as your greatest step towards success.

_____

Imagine Your Outcome.

What time of day did you perform this exercise? _____

Describe how you felt (using 2 words) prior to performing it: _____ & _____

Describe how you felt (using 2 words) after performing it: _____ & _____

List any challenges you had during the exercise:

_____

_____

_____

Describe two positive and memorable moments, thoughts, or feelings you experienced during the exercise:

_____

_____

_____

Hold the Vision. Trust the Process. Commit to Today.

Today's Date: _____

Learn My Language: What is my language telling me today?

_____

_____

_____

_____

Review My Direction:

Goal #1: _____

What are my reflections about this goal?

_____

_____

_____

_____

Goal #2: _____

What are my reflections about this goal?

_____

_____

_____

_____

Goal #3: _____

What are my reflections about this goal?

_____

_____

_____

_____

Count My Wins:

What did I do today that helped move me closer to achieving my goals? (List everything you can think of.)

_____

_____

_____

_____

_____

_____

_____

_____

My One Thing: Pick one win from above and isolate that as your greatest step towards success.

_____

Imagine Your Outcome.

What time of day did you perform this exercise? _____

Describe how you felt (using 2 words) prior to performing it: _____ & _____

Describe how you felt (using 2 words) after performing it: _____ & _____

List any challenges you had during the exercise:

_____

_____

_____

Describe two positive and memorable moments, thoughts, or feelings you experienced during the exercise:

_____

_____

_____

Hold the Vision. Trust the Process. Commit to Today.

Today's Date: _____

Learn My Language: What is my language telling me today?

_____

_____

_____

_____

Review My Direction:

Goal #1: _____

What are my reflections about this goal?

_____

_____

_____

_____

Goal #2: _____

What are my reflections about this goal?

_____

_____

_____

_____

Goal #3: _____

What are my reflections about this goal?

_____

_____

_____

_____

Count My Wins:

What did I do today that helped move me closer to achieving my goals? (List everything you can think of.)

_____

_____

_____

_____

_____

_____

_____

My One Thing: Pick one win from above and isolate that as your greatest step towards success.

_____

Imagine Your Outcome.

What time of day did you perform this exercise? _____

Describe how you felt (using 2 words) prior to performing it: _____ & _____

Describe how you felt (using 2 words) after performing it: _____ & _____

List any challenges you had during the exercise:

_____

_____

_____

Describe two positive and memorable moments, thoughts, or feelings you experienced during the exercise:

_____

_____

_____

Hold the Vision. Trust the Process. Commit to Today.

Today's Date: _____

Learn My Language: What is my language telling me today?

_____

_____

_____

_____

Review My Direction:

Goal #1: _____

What are my reflections about this goal?

_____

_____

_____

_____

Goal #2: _____

What are my reflections about this goal?

_____

_____

_____

_____

Goal #3: _____

What are my reflections about this goal?

_____

_____

_____

_____

Count My Wins:

What did I do today that helped move me closer to achieving my goals? (List everything you can think of.)

_____

_____

_____

_____

_____

_____

_____

_____

My One Thing: Pick one win from above and isolate that as your greatest step towards success.

_____

Imagine Your Outcome.

What time of day did you perform this exercise? _____

Describe how you felt (using 2 words) prior to performing it: _____ & _____

Describe how you felt (using 2 words) after performing it: _____ & _____

List any challenges you had during the exercise:

_____

_____

_____

Describe two positive and memorable moments, thoughts, or feelings you experienced during the exercise:

_____

_____

_____

Hold the Vision. Trust the Process. Commit to Today.

Today's Date: _____

Learn My Language: What is my language telling me today?

_____

_____

_____

_____

Review My Direction:

Goal #1: _____

What are my reflections about this goal?

_____

_____

_____

_____

Goal #2: _____

What are my reflections about this goal?

_____

_____

_____

_____

Goal #3: _____

What are my reflections about this goal?

_____

_____

_____

_____

Count My Wins:

What did I do today that helped move me closer to achieving my goals? (List everything you can think of.)

_____

_____

_____

_____

_____

_____

_____

_____

My One Thing: Pick one win from above and isolate that as your greatest step towards success.

_____

Imagine Your Outcome.

What time of day did you perform this exercise? _____

Describe how you felt (using 2 words) prior to performing it: _____ & _____

Describe how you felt (using 2 words) after performing it: _____ & _____

List any challenges you had during the exercise:

_____

_____

_____

Describe two positive and memorable moments, thoughts, or feelings you experienced during the exercise:

_____

_____

_____

Hold the Vision. Trust the Process. Commit to Today.

Today's Date: _____

Learn My Language: What is my language telling me today?

_____

_____

_____

_____

Review My Direction:

Goal #1: _____

What are my reflections about this goal?

_____

_____

_____

_____

Goal #2: _____

What are my reflections about this goal?

_____

_____

_____

_____

Goal #3: _____

What are my reflections about this goal?

_____

_____

_____

_____

BRIAN & CARRIE
LET'S ELIMINATE YOUR LIMITS
WWW.BRIANANDCARRIE.LIVE

Count My Wins:

What did I do today that helped move me closer to achieving my goals? (List everything you can think of.)

_____

_____

_____

_____

_____

_____

_____

_____

My One Thing: Pick one win from above and isolate that as your greatest step towards success.

_____

Imagine Your Outcome.

What time of day did you perform this exercise? _____

Describe how you felt (using 2 words) prior to performing it: _____ & _____

Describe how you felt (using 2 words) after performing it: _____ & _____

List any challenges you had during the exercise:

_____

_____

_____

Describe two positive and memorable moments, thoughts, or feelings you experienced during the exercise:

_____

_____

_____

Hold the Vision. Trust the Process. Commit to Today.

Today's Date: _____

Learn My Language: What is my language telling me today?

_____

_____

_____

_____

Review My Direction:

Goal #1: _____

What are my reflections about this goal?

_____

_____

_____

_____

Goal #2: _____

What are my reflections about this goal?

_____

_____

_____

_____

Goal #3: _____

What are my reflections about this goal?

_____

_____

_____

_____

Count My Wins:

What did I do today that helped move me closer to achieving my goals? (List everything you can think of.)

_____

_____

_____

_____

_____

_____

_____

_____

My One Thing: Pick one win from above and isolate that as your greatest step towards success.

_____

Imagine Your Outcome.

What time of day did you perform this exercise? _____

Describe how you felt (using 2 words) prior to performing it: _____ & _____

Describe how you felt (using 2 words) after performing it: _____ & _____

List any challenges you had during the exercise:

_____

_____

_____

Describe two positive and memorable moments, thoughts, or feelings you experienced during the exercise:

_____

_____

_____

Hold the Vision. Trust the Process. Commit to Today.

Today's Date: _____

Learn My Language: What is my language telling me today?

_____

_____

_____

_____

Review My Direction:

Goal #1: _____

What are my reflections about this goal?

_____

_____

_____

_____

Goal #2: _____

What are my reflections about this goal?

_____

_____

_____

_____

Goal #3: _____

What are my reflections about this goal?

_____

_____

_____

_____

Count My Wins:

What did I do today that helped move me closer to achieving my goals? (List everything you can think of.)

_____

_____

_____

_____

_____

_____

_____

_____

My One Thing: Pick one win from above and isolate that as your greatest step towards success.

_____

Imagine Your Outcome.

What time of day did you perform this exercise? _____

Describe how you felt (using 2 words) prior to performing it: _____ & _____

Describe how you felt (using 2 words) after performing it: _____ & _____

List any challenges you had during the exercise:

_____

_____

_____

Describe two positive and memorable moments, thoughts, or feelings you experienced during the exercise:

_____

_____

_____

Hold the Vision. Trust the Process. Commit to Today.

Today's Date: _____

Learn My Language: What is my language telling me today?

_____

_____

_____

_____

Review My Direction:

Goal #1: _____

What are my reflections about this goal?

_____

_____

_____

_____

Goal #2: _____

What are my reflections about this goal?

_____

_____

_____

_____

Goal #3: _____

What are my reflections about this goal?

_____

_____

_____

_____

Count My Wins:

What did I do today that helped move me closer to achieving my goals? (List everything you can think of.)

_____

_____

_____

_____

_____

_____

_____

_____

My One Thing: Pick one win from above and isolate that as your greatest step towards success.

_____

Imagine Your Outcome.

What time of day did you perform this exercise? _____

Describe how you felt (using 2 words) prior to performing it: _____ & _____

Describe how you felt (using 2 words) after performing it: _____ & _____

List any challenges you had during the exercise:

_____

_____

_____

Describe two positive and memorable moments, thoughts, or feelings you experienced during the exercise:

_____

_____

_____

Hold the Vision. Trust the Process. Commit to Today.

Today's Date: _____

Learn My Language: What is my language telling me today?

_____

_____

_____

_____

Review My Direction:

Goal #1: _____

What are my reflections about this goal?

_____

_____

_____

_____

Goal #2: _____

What are my reflections about this goal?

_____

_____

_____

_____

Goal #3: _____

What are my reflections about this goal?

_____

_____

_____

_____

Count My Wins:

What did I do today that helped move me closer to achieving my goals? (List everything you can think of.)

_____

_____

_____

_____

_____

_____

_____

My One Thing: Pick one win from above and isolate that as your greatest step towards success.

_____

Imagine Your Outcome.

What time of day did you perform this exercise? _____

Describe how you felt (using 2 words) prior to performing it: _____ & _____

Describe how you felt (using 2 words) after performing it: _____ & _____

List any challenges you had during the exercise:

_____

_____

_____

Describe two positive and memorable moments, thoughts, or feelings you experienced during the exercise:

_____

_____

_____

Hold the Vision. Trust the Process. Commit to Today.

Today's Date: _____

Learn My Language: What is my language telling me today?

_____

_____

_____

_____

Review My Direction:

Goal #1: _____

What are my reflections about this goal?

_____

_____

_____

_____

Goal #2: _____

What are my reflections about this goal?

_____

_____

_____

_____

Goal #3: _____

What are my reflections about this goal?

_____

_____

_____

_____

Count My Wins:

What did I do today that helped move me closer to achieving my goals? (List everything you can think of.)

_____

_____

_____

_____

_____

_____

_____

_____

My One Thing: Pick one win from above and isolate that as your greatest step towards success.

_____

Imagine Your Outcome.

What time of day did you perform this exercise? _____

Describe how you felt (using 2 words) prior to performing it: _____ & _____

Describe how you felt (using 2 words) after performing it: _____ & _____

List any challenges you had during the exercise:

_____

_____

_____

Describe two positive and memorable moments, thoughts, or feelings you experienced during the exercise:

_____

_____

_____

Hold the Vision. Trust the Process. Commit to Today.

Today's Date: _____

Learn My Language: What is my language telling me today?

_____

_____

_____

_____

Review My Direction:

Goal #1: _____

What are my reflections about this goal?

_____

_____

_____

_____

Goal #2: _____

What are my reflections about this goal?

_____

_____

_____

_____

Goal #3: _____

What are my reflections about this goal?

_____

_____

_____

_____

Count My Wins:

What did I do today that helped move me closer to achieving my goals? (List everything you can think of.)

_____

_____

_____

_____

_____

_____

_____

_____

My One Thing: Pick one win from above and isolate that as your greatest step towards success.

_____

Imagine Your Outcome.

What time of day did you perform this exercise? _____

Describe how you felt (using 2 words) prior to performing it: _____ & _____

Describe how you felt (using 2 words) after performing it: _____ & _____

List any challenges you had during the exercise:

_____

_____

_____

Describe two positive and memorable moments, thoughts, or feelings you experienced during the exercise:

_____

_____

_____

Hold the Vision. Trust the Process. Commit to Today.

Today's Date: _____

Learn My Language: What is my language telling me today?

_____

_____

_____

_____

Review My Direction:

Goal #1: _____

What are my reflections about this goal?

_____

_____

_____

_____

Goal #2: _____

What are my reflections about this goal?

_____

_____

_____

_____

Goal #3: _____

What are my reflections about this goal?

_____

_____

_____

_____

Count My Wins:

What did I do today that helped move me closer to achieving my goals? (List everything you can think of.)

_____

_____

_____

_____

_____

_____

_____

_____

My One Thing: Pick one win from above and isolate that as your greatest step towards success.

_____

Imagine Your Outcome.

What time of day did you perform this exercise? _____

Describe how you felt (using 2 words) prior to performing it: _____ & _____

Describe how you felt (using 2 words) after performing it: _____ & _____

List any challenges you had during the exercise:

_____

_____

_____

Describe two positive and memorable moments, thoughts, or feelings you experienced during the exercise:

_____

_____

_____

Hold the Vision. Trust the Process. Commit to Today.

BRIAN & CARRIE
LET'S ELIMINATE YOUR LIMITS
WWW.BRIANANDCARRIE.LIVE

Today's Date: _____

Learn My Language: What is my language telling me today?

_____

_____

_____

_____

Review My Direction:

Goal #1: _____

What are my reflections about this goal?

_____

_____

_____

_____

Goal #2: _____

What are my reflections about this goal?

_____

_____

_____

_____

Goal #3: _____

What are my reflections about this goal?

_____

_____

_____

_____

Count My Wins:

What did I do today that helped move me closer to achieving my goals? (List everything you can think of.)

_____

_____

_____

_____

_____

_____

_____

_____

My One Thing: Pick one win from above and isolate that as your greatest step towards success.

_____

Imagine Your Outcome.

What time of day did you perform this exercise? _____

Describe how you felt (using 2 words) prior to performing it: _____ & _____

Describe how you felt (using 2 words) after performing it: _____ & _____

List any challenges you had during the exercise:

_____

_____

_____

Describe two positive and memorable moments, thoughts, or feelings you experienced during the exercise:

_____

_____

_____

Hold the Vision. Trust the Process. Commit to Today.

Today's Date: _____

Learn My Language: What is my language telling me today?

_____
_____
_____
_____

Review My Direction:

Goal #1: _____

What are my reflections about this goal?

_____
_____
_____
_____

Goal #2: _____

What are my reflections about this goal?

_____
_____
_____
_____

Goal #3: _____

What are my reflections about this goal?

_____
_____
_____
_____

Count My Wins:

What did I do today that helped move me closer to achieving my goals? (List everything you can think of.)

_____

_____

_____

_____

_____

_____

_____

_____

My One Thing: Pick one win from above and isolate that as your greatest step towards success.

_____

Imagine Your Outcome.

What time of day did you perform this exercise? _____

Describe how you felt (using 2 words) prior to performing it: _____ & _____

Describe how you felt (using 2 words) after performing it: _____ & _____

List any challenges you had during the exercise:

_____

_____

_____

Describe two positive and memorable moments, thoughts, or feelings you experienced during the exercise:

_____

_____

_____

Hold the Vision. Trust the Process. Commit to Today.

BRIAN & CARRIE
LET'S ELIMINATE YOUR LIMITS
WWW.BRIANANDCARRIE.LIVE

Today's Date: _____

Learn My Language: What is my language telling me today?

_____

_____

_____

_____

Review My Direction:

Goal #1: _____

What are my reflections about this goal?

_____

_____

_____

_____

Goal #2: _____

What are my reflections about this goal?

_____

_____

_____

_____

Goal #3: _____

What are my reflections about this goal?

_____

_____

_____

_____

Count My Wins:

What did I do today that helped move me closer to achieving my goals? (List everything you can think of.)

_____

_____

_____

_____

_____

_____

_____

_____

My One Thing: Pick one win from above and isolate that as your greatest step towards success.

_____

Imagine Your Outcome.

What time of day did you perform this exercise? _____

Describe how you felt (using 2 words) prior to performing it: _____ & _____

Describe how you felt (using 2 words) after performing it: _____ & _____

List any challenges you had during the exercise:

_____

_____

_____

Describe two positive and memorable moments, thoughts, or feelings you experienced during the exercise:

_____

_____

_____

Hold the Vision. Trust the Process. Commit to Today.

Today's Date: _____

Learn My Language: What is my language telling me today?

_____

_____

_____

_____

Review My Direction:

Goal #1: _____

What are my reflections about this goal?

_____

_____

_____

_____

Goal #2: _____

What are my reflections about this goal?

_____

_____

_____

_____

Goal #3: _____

What are my reflections about this goal?

_____

_____

_____

_____

Count My Wins:

What did I do today that helped move me closer to achieving my goals? (List everything you can think of.)

_____

_____

_____

_____

_____

_____

_____

_____

My One Thing: Pick one win from above and isolate that as your greatest step towards success.

_____

Imagine Your Outcome.

What time of day did you perform this exercise? _____

Describe how you felt (using 2 words) prior to performing it: _____ & _____

Describe how you felt (using 2 words) after performing it: _____ & _____

List any challenges you had during the exercise:

_____

_____

_____

Describe two positive and memorable moments, thoughts, or feelings you experienced during the exercise:

_____

_____

_____

Hold the Vision. Trust the Process. Commit to Today.

BRIAN & CARRIE
LET'S ELIMINATE YOUR LIMITS
WWW.BRIANANDCARRIE.LIVE

Today's Date: _____

Learn My Language: What is my language telling me today?

_____

_____

_____

_____

Review My Direction:

Goal #1: _____

What are my reflections about this goal?

_____

_____

_____

_____

Goal #2: _____

What are my reflections about this goal?

_____

_____

_____

_____

Goal #3: _____

What are my reflections about this goal?

_____

_____

_____

_____

Count My Wins:

What did I do today that helped move me closer to achieving my goals? (List everything you can think of.)

_____

_____

_____

_____

_____

_____

_____

_____

My One Thing: Pick one win from above and isolate that as your greatest step towards success.

_____

Imagine Your Outcome.

What time of day did you perform this exercise? _____

Describe how you felt (using 2 words) prior to performing it: _____ & _____

Describe how you felt (using 2 words) after performing it: _____ & _____

List any challenges you had during the exercise:

_____

_____

Describe two positive and memorable moments, thoughts, or feelings you experienced during the exercise:

_____

_____

_____

Hold the Vision. Trust the Process. Commit to Today.

Today's Date: _____

Learn My Language: What is my language telling me today?

_____

_____

_____

_____

Review My Direction:

Goal #1: _____

What are my reflections about this goal?

_____

_____

_____

_____

Goal #2: _____

What are my reflections about this goal?

_____

_____

_____

_____

Goal #3: _____

What are my reflections about this goal?

_____

_____

_____

_____

Count My Wins:

What did I do today that helped move me closer to achieving my goals? (List everything you can think of.)

_____

_____

_____

_____

_____

_____

_____

_____

_____

My One Thing: Pick one win from above and isolate that as your greatest step towards success.

_____

Imagine Your Outcome.

What time of day did you perform this exercise? _____

Describe how you felt (using 2 words) prior to performing it: _____ & _____

Describe how you felt (using 2 words) after performing it: _____ & _____

List any challenges you had during the exercise:

_____

_____

_____

Describe two positive and memorable moments, thoughts, or feelings you experienced during the exercise:

_____

_____

_____

Hold the Vision. Trust the Process. Commit to Today.

Today's Date: _____

Learn My Language: What is my language telling me today?

_____

_____

_____

_____

Review My Direction:

Goal #1: _____

What are my reflections about this goal?

_____

_____

_____

_____

Goal #2: _____

What are my reflections about this goal?

_____

_____

_____

_____

Goal #3: _____

What are my reflections about this goal?

_____

_____

_____

_____

Count My Wins:

What did I do today that helped move me closer to achieving my goals? (List everything you can think of.)

_____

_____

_____

_____

_____

_____

_____

My One Thing: Pick one win from above and isolate that as your greatest step towards success.

_____

Imagine Your Outcome.

What time of day did you perform this exercise? _____

Describe how you felt (using 2 words) prior to performing it: _____ & _____

Describe how you felt (using 2 words) after performing it: _____ & _____

List any challenges you had during the exercise:

_____

_____

Describe two positive and memorable moments, thoughts, or feelings you experienced during the exercise:

_____

_____

_____

Hold the Vision. Trust the Process. Commit to Today.

Today's Date: _____

Learn My Language: What is my language telling me today?

_____

_____

_____

_____

Review My Direction:

Goal #1: _____

What are my reflections about this goal?

_____

_____

_____

_____

Goal #2: _____

What are my reflections about this goal?

_____

_____

_____

_____

Goal #3: _____

What are my reflections about this goal?

_____

_____

_____

_____

Count My Wins:

What did I do today that helped move me closer to achieving my goals? (List everything you can think of.)

_____

_____

_____

_____

_____

_____

_____

_____

My One Thing: Pick one win from above and isolate that as your greatest step towards success.

_____

Imagine Your Outcome.

What time of day did you perform this exercise? _____

Describe how you felt (using 2 words) prior to performing it: _____ & _____

Describe how you felt (using 2 words) after performing it: _____ & _____

List any challenges you had during the exercise:

_____

_____

_____

Describe two positive and memorable moments, thoughts, or feelings you experienced during the exercise:

_____

_____

_____

Hold the Vision. Trust the Process. Commit to Today.

BRIAN & CARRIE
LET'S ELIMINATE YOUR LIMITS
WWW.BRIANANDCARRIE.LIVE

Today's Date: _____

Learn My Language: What is my language telling me today?

_____

_____

_____

_____

Review My Direction:

Goal #1: _____

What are my reflections about this goal?

_____

_____

_____

_____

Goal #2: _____

What are my reflections about this goal?

_____

_____

_____

_____

Goal #3: _____

What are my reflections about this goal?

_____

_____

_____

_____

Count My Wins:

What did I do today that helped move me closer to achieving my goals? (List everything you can think of.)

_____

_____

_____

_____

_____

_____

_____

My One Thing: Pick one win from above and isolate that as your greatest step towards success.

_____

Imagine Your Outcome.

What time of day did you perform this exercise? _____

Describe how you felt (using 2 words) prior to performing it: _____ & _____

Describe how you felt (using 2 words) after performing it: _____ & _____

List any challenges you had during the exercise:

_____

_____

_____

Describe two positive and memorable moments, thoughts, or feelings you experienced during the exercise:

_____

_____

_____

Hold the Vision. Trust the Process. Commit to Today.

Today's Date: _____

Learn My Language: What is my language telling me today?

_____

_____

_____

_____

Review My Direction:

Goal #1: _____

What are my reflections about this goal?

_____

_____

_____

_____

Goal #2: _____

What are my reflections about this goal?

_____

_____

_____

_____

Goal #3: _____

What are my reflections about this goal?

_____

_____

_____

_____

BRIAN & CARRIE
LET'S ELIMINATE YOUR LIMITS
WWW.BRIANANDCARRIE.LIVE

Count My Wins:

What did I do today that helped move me closer to achieving my goals? (List everything you can think of.)

_____

_____

_____

_____

_____

_____

_____

My One Thing: Pick one win from above and isolate that as your greatest step towards success.

_____

Imagine Your Outcome.

What time of day did you perform this exercise? _____

Describe how you felt (using 2 words) prior to performing it: _____ & _____

Describe how you felt (using 2 words) after performing it: _____ & _____

List any challenges you had during the exercise:

_____

_____

_____

Describe two positive and memorable moments, thoughts, or feelings you experienced during the exercise:

_____

_____

_____

Hold the Vision. Trust the Process. Commit to Today.

Today's Date: _____

Learn My Language: What is my language telling me today?

_____
_____
_____
_____

Review My Direction:

Goal #1: _____

What are my reflections about this goal?

_____
_____
_____
_____

Goal #2: _____

What are my reflections about this goal?

_____
_____
_____
_____

Goal #3: _____

What are my reflections about this goal?

_____
_____
_____
_____

Count My Wins:

What did I do today that helped move me closer to achieving my goals? (List everything you can think of.)

_____

_____

_____

_____

_____

_____

_____

My One Thing: Pick one win from above and isolate that as your greatest step towards success.

_____

Imagine Your Outcome.

What time of day did you perform this exercise? _____

Describe how you felt (using 2 words) prior to performing it: _____ & _____

Describe how you felt (using 2 words) after performing it: _____ & _____

List any challenges you had during the exercise:

_____

_____

Describe two positive and memorable moments, thoughts, or feelings you experienced during the exercise:

_____

_____

_____

Hold the Vision. Trust the Process. Commit to Today.

Today's Date: _____

Learn My Language: What is my language telling me today?

_____

_____

_____

_____

Review My Direction:

Goal #1: _____

What are my reflections about this goal?

_____

_____

_____

_____

Goal #2: _____

What are my reflections about this goal?

_____

_____

_____

_____

Goal #3: _____

What are my reflections about this goal?

_____

_____

_____

_____

Count My Wins:

What did I do today that helped move me closer to achieving my goals? (List everything you can think of.)

_____

_____

_____

_____

_____

_____

_____

_____

My One Thing: Pick one win from above and isolate that as your greatest step towards success.

_____

Imagine Your Outcome.

What time of day did you perform this exercise? _____

Describe how you felt (using 2 words) prior to performing it: _____ & _____

Describe how you felt (using 2 words) after performing it: _____ & _____

List any challenges you had during the exercise:

_____

_____

_____

Describe two positive and memorable moments, thoughts, or feelings you experienced during the exercise:

_____

_____

_____

Hold the Vision. Trust the Process. Commit to Today.

BRIAN & CARRIE
LET'S ELIMINATE YOUR LIMITS
WWW.BRIANANDCARRIE.LIVE

Today's Date: _____

Learn My Language: What is my language telling me today?

_____
_____
_____
_____

Review My Direction:

Goal #1: _____

What are my reflections about this goal?

_____
_____
_____
_____

Goal #2: _____

What are my reflections about this goal?

_____
_____
_____
_____

Goal #3: _____

What are my reflections about this goal?

_____
_____
_____
_____

Count My Wins:

What did I do today that helped move me closer to achieving my goals? (List everything you can think of.)

_____

_____

_____

_____

_____

_____

_____

_____

My One Thing: Pick one win from above and isolate that as your greatest step towards success.

_____

Imagine Your Outcome.

What time of day did you perform this exercise? _____

Describe how you felt (using 2 words) prior to performing it: _____ & _____

Describe how you felt (using 2 words) after performing it: _____ & _____

List any challenges you had during the exercise:

_____

_____

_____

Describe two positive and memorable moments, thoughts, or feelings you experienced during the exercise:

_____

_____

_____

Hold the Vision. Trust the Process. Commit to Today.

Today's Date: _____

Learn My Language: What is my language telling me today?

_____

_____

_____

_____

Review My Direction:

Goal #1: _____

What are my reflections about this goal?

_____

_____

_____

_____

Goal #2: _____

What are my reflections about this goal?

_____

_____

_____

_____

Goal #3: _____

What are my reflections about this goal?

_____

_____

_____

_____

Count My Wins:

What did I do today that helped move me closer to achieving my goals? (List everything you can think of.)

_____

_____

_____

_____

_____

_____

_____

_____

My One Thing: Pick one win from above and isolate that as your greatest step towards success.

_____

Imagine Your Outcome.

What time of day did you perform this exercise? _____

Describe how you felt (using 2 words) prior to performing it: _____ & _____

Describe how you felt (using 2 words) after performing it: _____ & _____

List any challenges you had during the exercise:

_____

_____

_____

Describe two positive and memorable moments, thoughts, or feelings you experienced during the exercise:

_____

_____

_____

Hold the Vision. Trust the Process. Commit to Today.

Today's Date: _____

Learn My Language: What is my language telling me today?

_____

_____

_____

_____

Review My Direction:

Goal #1: _____

What are my reflections about this goal?

_____

_____

_____

_____

Goal #2: _____

What are my reflections about this goal?

_____

_____

_____

_____

Goal #3: _____

What are my reflections about this goal?

_____

_____

_____

_____

Count My Wins:

What did I do today that helped move me closer to achieving my goals? (List everything you can think of.)

_____

_____

_____

_____

_____

_____

_____

_____

My One Thing: Pick one win from above and isolate that as your greatest step towards success.

_____

Imagine Your Outcome.

What time of day did you perform this exercise? _____

Describe how you felt (using 2 words) prior to performing it: _____ & _____

Describe how you felt (using 2 words) after performing it: _____ & _____

List any challenges you had during the exercise:

_____

_____

_____

Describe two positive and memorable moments, thoughts, or feelings you experienced during the exercise:

_____

_____

_____

Hold the Vision. Trust the Process. Commit to Today.

Today's Date: _____

Learn My Language: What is my language telling me today?

_____

_____

_____

_____

Review My Direction:

Goal #1: _____

What are my reflections about this goal?

_____

_____

_____

_____

Goal #2: _____

What are my reflections about this goal?

_____

_____

_____

_____

Goal #3: _____

What are my reflections about this goal?

_____

_____

_____

_____

Count My Wins:

What did I do today that helped move me closer to achieving my goals? (List everything you can think of.)

_____

_____

_____

_____

_____

_____

_____

_____

My One Thing: Pick one win from above and isolate that as your greatest step towards success.

_____

Imagine Your Outcome.

What time of day did you perform this exercise? _____

Describe how you felt (using 2 words) prior to performing it: _____ & _____

Describe how you felt (using 2 words) after performing it: _____ & _____

List any challenges you had during the exercise:

_____

_____

_____

Describe two positive and memorable moments, thoughts, or feelings you experienced during the exercise:

_____

_____

_____

Hold the Vision. Trust the Process. Commit to Today.

Today's Date: _____

Learn My Language: What is my language telling me today?

_____

_____

_____

_____

Review My Direction:

Goal #1: _____

What are my reflections about this goal?

_____

_____

_____

_____

Goal #2: _____

What are my reflections about this goal?

_____

_____

_____

_____

Goal #3: _____

What are my reflections about this goal?

_____

_____

_____

_____

Count My Wins:

What did I do today that helped move me closer to achieving my goals? (List everything you can think of.)

_____

_____

_____

_____

_____

_____

_____

_____

My One Thing: Pick one win from above and isolate that as your greatest step towards success.

_____

Imagine Your Outcome.

What time of day did you perform this exercise? _____

Describe how you felt (using 2 words) prior to performing it: _____ & _____

Describe how you felt (using 2 words) after performing it: _____ & _____

List any challenges you had during the exercise:

_____

_____

_____

Describe two positive and memorable moments, thoughts, or feelings you experienced during the exercise:

_____

_____

_____

Hold the Vision. Trust the Process. Commit to Today.

Today's Date: _____

Learn My Language: What is my language telling me today?

_____

_____

_____

_____

Review My Direction:

Goal #1: _____

What are my reflections about this goal?

_____

_____

_____

_____

Goal #2: _____

What are my reflections about this goal?

_____

_____

_____

_____

Goal #3: _____

What are my reflections about this goal?

_____

_____

_____

_____

Count My Wins:

What did I do today that helped move me closer to achieving my goals? (List everything you can think of.)

_____

_____

_____

_____

_____

_____

_____

_____

My One Thing: Pick one win from above and isolate that as your greatest step towards success.

_____

Imagine Your Outcome.

What time of day did you perform this exercise? _____

Describe how you felt (using 2 words) prior to performing it: _____ & _____

Describe how you felt (using 2 words) after performing it: _____ & _____

List any challenges you had during the exercise:

_____

_____

_____

Describe two positive and memorable moments, thoughts, or feelings you experienced during the exercise:

_____

_____

_____

Hold the Vision. Trust the Process. Commit to Today.

Today's Date: _____

Learn My Language: What is my language telling me today?

_____

_____

_____

_____

Review My Direction:

Goal #1: _____

What are my reflections about this goal?

_____

_____

_____

_____

Goal #2: _____

What are my reflections about this goal?

_____

_____

_____

_____

Goal #3: _____

What are my reflections about this goal?

_____

_____

_____

_____

Count My Wins:

What did I do today that helped move me closer to achieving my goals? (List everything you can think of.)

_____

_____

_____

_____

_____

_____

_____

_____

My One Thing: Pick one win from above and isolate that as your greatest step towards success.

_____

Imagine Your Outcome.

What time of day did you perform this exercise? _____

Describe how you felt (using 2 words) prior to performing it: _____ & _____

Describe how you felt (using 2 words) after performing it: _____ & _____

List any challenges you had during the exercise:

_____

_____

_____

Describe two positive and memorable moments, thoughts, or feelings you experienced during the exercise:

_____

_____

_____

Hold the Vision. Trust the Process. Commit to Today.

Today's Date: _____

Learn My Language: What is my language telling me today?

_____

_____

_____

_____

Review My Direction:

Goal #1: _____

What are my reflections about this goal?

_____

_____

_____

_____

Goal #2: _____

What are my reflections about this goal?

_____

_____

_____

_____

Goal #3: _____

What are my reflections about this goal?

_____

_____

_____

_____

Count My Wins:

What did I do today that helped move me closer to achieving my goals? (List everything you can think of.)

_____

_____

_____

_____

_____

_____

_____

_____

My One Thing: Pick one win from above and isolate that as your greatest step towards success.

_____

Imagine Your Outcome.

What time of day did you perform this exercise? _____

Describe how you felt (using 2 words) prior to performing it: _____ & _____

Describe how you felt (using 2 words) after performing it: _____ & _____

List any challenges you had during the exercise:

_____

_____

_____

Describe two positive and memorable moments, thoughts, or feelings you experienced during the exercise:

_____

_____

_____

Hold the Vision. Trust the Process. Commit to Today.

Today's Date: _____

Learn My Language: What is my language telling me today?

_____

_____

_____

_____

Review My Direction:

Goal #1: _____

What are my reflections about this goal?

_____

_____

_____

_____

Goal #2: _____

What are my reflections about this goal?

_____

_____

_____

_____

Goal #3: _____

What are my reflections about this goal?

_____

_____

_____

_____

Count My Wins:

What did I do today that helped move me closer to achieving my goals? (List everything you can think of.)

_____

_____

_____

_____

_____

_____

_____

_____

My One Thing: Pick one win from above and isolate that as your greatest step towards success.

_____

Imagine Your Outcome.

What time of day did you perform this exercise? _____

Describe how you felt (using 2 words) prior to performing it: _____ & _____

Describe how you felt (using 2 words) after performing it: _____ & _____

List any challenges you had during the exercise:

_____

_____

_____

Describe two positive and memorable moments, thoughts, or feelings you experienced during the exercise:

_____

_____

_____

Hold the Vision. Trust the Process. Commit to Today.

Today's Date: _____

Learn My Language: What is my language telling me today?

_____

_____

_____

_____

Review My Direction:

Goal #1: _____

What are my reflections about this goal?

_____

_____

_____

_____

Goal #2: _____

What are my reflections about this goal?

_____

_____

_____

_____

Goal #3: _____

What are my reflections about this goal?

_____

_____

_____

_____

Count My Wins:

What did I do today that helped move me closer to achieving my goals? (List everything you can think of.)

_____

_____

_____

_____

_____

_____

_____

_____

My One Thing: Pick one win from above and isolate that as your greatest step towards success.

_____

Imagine Your Outcome.

What time of day did you perform this exercise? _____

Describe how you felt (using 2 words) prior to performing it: _____ & _____

Describe how you felt (using 2 words) after performing it: _____ & _____

List any challenges you had during the exercise:

_____

_____

_____

Describe two positive and memorable moments, thoughts, or feelings you experienced during the exercise:

_____

_____

_____

Hold the Vision. Trust the Process. Commit to Today.

Today's Date: _____

Learn My Language: What is my language telling me today?

_____

_____

_____

_____

Review My Direction:

Goal #1: _____

What are my reflections about this goal?

_____

_____

_____

_____

Goal #2: _____

What are my reflections about this goal?

_____

_____

_____

_____

Goal #3: _____

What are my reflections about this goal?

_____

_____

_____

_____

Count My Wins:

What did I do today that helped move me closer to achieving my goals? (List everything you can think of.)

_____

_____

_____

_____

_____

_____

_____

_____

My One Thing: Pick one win from above and isolate that as your greatest step towards success.

_____

Imagine Your Outcome.

What time of day did you perform this exercise? _____

Describe how you felt (using 2 words) prior to performing it: _____ & _____

Describe how you felt (using 2 words) after performing it: _____ & _____

List any challenges you had during the exercise:

_____

_____

Describe two positive and memorable moments, thoughts, or feelings you experienced during the exercise:

_____

_____

_____

Hold the Vision. Trust the Process. Commit to Today.

Today's Date: _____

Learn My Language: What is my language telling me today?

_____

_____

_____

_____

Review My Direction:

Goal #1: _____

What are my reflections about this goal?

_____

_____

_____

_____

Goal #2: _____

What are my reflections about this goal?

_____

_____

_____

_____

Goal #3: _____

What are my reflections about this goal?

_____

_____

_____

_____

Count My Wins:

What did I do today that helped move me closer to achieving my goals? (List everything you can think of.)

_____

_____

_____

_____

_____

_____

_____

_____

My One Thing: Pick one win from above and isolate that as your greatest step towards success.

_____

Imagine Your Outcome.

What time of day did you perform this exercise? _____

Describe how you felt (using 2 words) prior to performing it: _____ & _____

Describe how you felt (using 2 words) after performing it: _____ & _____

List any challenges you had during the exercise:

_____

_____

_____

Describe two positive and memorable moments, thoughts, or feelings you experienced during the exercise:

_____

_____

_____

Hold the Vision. Trust the Process. Commit to Today.

Today's Date: _____

Learn My Language: What is my language telling me today?

_____

_____

_____

_____

Review My Direction:

Goal #1: _____

What are my reflections about this goal?

_____

_____

_____

_____

Goal #2: _____

What are my reflections about this goal?

_____

_____

_____

_____

Goal #3: _____

What are my reflections about this goal?

_____

_____

_____

_____

Count My Wins:

What did I do today that helped move me closer to achieving my goals? (List everything you can think of.)

_____

_____

_____

_____

_____

_____

_____

_____

My One Thing: Pick one win from above and isolate that as your greatest step towards success.

_____

Imagine Your Outcome.

What time of day did you perform this exercise? _____

Describe how you felt (using 2 words) prior to performing it: _____ & _____

Describe how you felt (using 2 words) after performing it: _____ & _____

List any challenges you had during the exercise:

_____

_____

_____

Describe two positive and memorable moments, thoughts, or feelings you experienced during the exercise:

_____

_____

_____

Hold the Vision. Trust the Process. Commit to Today.

Today's Date: _____

Learn My Language: What is my language telling me today?

_____

_____

_____

_____

Review My Direction:

Goal #1: _____

What are my reflections about this goal?

_____

_____

_____

_____

Goal #2: _____

What are my reflections about this goal?

_____

_____

_____

_____

Goal #3: _____

What are my reflections about this goal?

_____

_____

_____

_____

Count My Wins:

What did I do today that helped move me closer to achieving my goals? (List everything you can think of.)

_____

_____

_____

_____

_____

_____

_____

_____

My One Thing: Pick one win from above and isolate that as your greatest step towards success.

_____

Imagine Your Outcome.

What time of day did you perform this exercise? _____

Describe how you felt (using 2 words) prior to performing it: _____ & _____

Describe how you felt (using 2 words) after performing it: _____ & _____

List any challenges you had during the exercise:

_____

_____

_____

Describe two positive and memorable moments, thoughts, or feelings you experienced during the exercise:

_____

_____

_____

Hold the Vision. Trust the Process. Commit to Today.

Today's Date: _____

Learn My Language: What is my language telling me today?

_____

_____

_____

_____

Review My Direction:

Goal #1: _____

What are my reflections about this goal?

_____

_____

_____

_____

Goal #2: _____

What are my reflections about this goal?

_____

_____

_____

_____

Goal #3: _____

What are my reflections about this goal?

_____

_____

_____

_____

Count My Wins:

What did I do today that helped move me closer to achieving my goals? (List everything you can think of.)

_____

_____

_____

_____

_____

_____

_____

_____

My One Thing: Pick one win from above and isolate that as your greatest step towards success.

_____

Imagine Your Outcome.

What time of day did you perform this exercise? _____

Describe how you felt (using 2 words) prior to performing it: _____ & _____

Describe how you felt (using 2 words) after performing it: _____ & _____

List any challenges you had during the exercise:

_____

_____

Describe two positive and memorable moments, thoughts, or feelings you experienced during the exercise:

_____

_____

Hold the Vision. Trust the Process. Commit to Today.

Today's Date: _____

Learn My Language: What is my language telling me today?

_____

_____

_____

_____

Review My Direction:

Goal #1: _____

What are my reflections about this goal?

_____

_____

_____

_____

Goal #2: _____

What are my reflections about this goal?

_____

_____

_____

_____

Goal #3: _____

What are my reflections about this goal?

_____

_____

_____

_____

Count My Wins:

What did I do today that helped move me closer to achieving my goals? (List everything you can think of.)

_____

_____

_____

_____

_____

_____

_____

_____

My One Thing: Pick one win from above and isolate that as your greatest step towards success.

_____

Imagine Your Outcome.

What time of day did you perform this exercise? _____

Describe how you felt (using 2 words) prior to performing it: _____ & _____

Describe how you felt (using 2 words) after performing it: _____ & _____

List any challenges you had during the exercise:

_____

_____

Describe two positive and memorable moments, thoughts, or feelings you experienced during the exercise:

_____

_____

_____

Hold the Vision. Trust the Process. Commit to Today.

Today's Date: _____

Learn My Language: What is my language telling me today?

_____

_____

_____

_____

Review My Direction:

Goal #1: _____

What are my reflections about this goal?

_____

_____

_____

_____

Goal #2: _____

What are my reflections about this goal?

_____

_____

_____

_____

Goal #3: _____

What are my reflections about this goal?

_____

_____

_____

_____

Count My Wins:

What did I do today that helped move me closer to achieving my goals? (List everything you can think of.)

_____

_____

_____

_____

_____

_____

_____

_____

My One Thing: Pick one win from above and isolate that as your greatest step towards success.

_____

Imagine Your Outcome.

What time of day did you perform this exercise? _____

Describe how you felt (using 2 words) prior to performing it: _____ & _____

Describe how you felt (using 2 words) after performing it: _____ & _____

List any challenges you had during the exercise:

_____

_____

_____

Describe two positive and memorable moments, thoughts, or feelings you experienced during the exercise:

_____

_____

_____

Hold the Vision. Trust the Process. Commit to Today.

Today's Date: _____

Learn My Language: What is my language telling me today?

_____

_____

_____

_____

Review My Direction:

Goal #1: _____

What are my reflections about this goal?

_____

_____

_____

_____

Goal #2: _____

What are my reflections about this goal?

_____

_____

_____

_____

Goal #3: _____

What are my reflections about this goal?

_____

_____

_____

_____

Count My Wins:

What did I do today that helped move me closer to achieving my goals? (List everything you can think of.)

_____

_____

_____

_____

_____

_____

_____

_____

My One Thing: Pick one win from above and isolate that as your greatest step towards success.

_____

Imagine Your Outcome.

What time of day did you perform this exercise? _____

Describe how you felt (using 2 words) prior to performing it: _____ & _____

Describe how you felt (using 2 words) after performing it: _____ & _____

List any challenges you had during the exercise:

_____

_____

Describe two positive and memorable moments, thoughts, or feelings you experienced during the exercise:

_____

_____

_____

Hold the Vision. Trust the Process. Commit to Today.

Today's Date: _____

Learn My Language: What is my language telling me today?

_____

_____

_____

_____

Review My Direction:

Goal #1: _____

What are my reflections about this goal?

_____

_____

_____

_____

Goal #2: _____

What are my reflections about this goal?

_____

_____

_____

_____

Goal #3: _____

What are my reflections about this goal?

_____

_____

_____

_____

Count My Wins:

What did I do today that helped move me closer to achieving my goals? (List everything you can think of.)

_____

_____

_____

_____

_____

_____

_____

_____

My One Thing: Pick one win from above and isolate that as your greatest step towards success.

_____

Imagine Your Outcome.

What time of day did you perform this exercise? _____

Describe how you felt (using 2 words) prior to performing it: _____ & _____

Describe how you felt (using 2 words) after performing it: _____ & _____

List any challenges you had during the exercise:

_____

_____

Describe two positive and memorable moments, thoughts, or feelings you experienced during the exercise:

_____

_____

_____

Hold the Vision. Trust the Process. Commit to Today.

BRIAN & CARRIE
LET'S ELIMINATE YOUR LIMITS
WWW.BRIANANDCARRIE.LIVE

Today's Date: _____

Learn My Language: What is my language telling me today?

_____

_____

_____

_____

Review My Direction:

Goal #1: _____

What are my reflections about this goal?

_____

_____

_____

_____

Goal #2: _____

What are my reflections about this goal?

_____

_____

_____

_____

Goal #3: _____

What are my reflections about this goal?

_____

_____

_____

_____

Count My Wins:

What did I do today that helped move me closer to achieving my goals? (List everything you can think of.)

_____

_____

_____

_____

_____

_____

_____

_____

My One Thing: Pick one win from above and isolate that as your greatest step towards success.

_____

Imagine Your Outcome.

What time of day did you perform this exercise? _____

Describe how you felt (using 2 words) prior to performing it: _____ & _____

Describe how you felt (using 2 words) after performing it: _____ & _____

List any challenges you had during the exercise:

_____

_____

Describe two positive and memorable moments, thoughts, or feelings you experienced during the exercise:

_____

_____

_____

Hold the Vision. Trust the Process. Commit to Today.

Today's Date: _____

Learn My Language: What is my language telling me today?

_____

_____

_____

_____

Review My Direction:

Goal #1: _____

What are my reflections about this goal?

_____

_____

_____

_____

Goal #2: _____

What are my reflections about this goal?

_____

_____

_____

_____

Goal #3: _____

What are my reflections about this goal?

_____

_____

_____

_____

Count My Wins:

What did I do today that helped move me closer to achieving my goals? (List everything you can think of.)

_____

_____

_____

_____

_____

_____

_____

_____

My One Thing: Pick one win from above and isolate that as your greatest step towards success.

_____

Imagine Your Outcome.

What time of day did you perform this exercise? _____

Describe how you felt (using 2 words) prior to performing it: _____ & _____

Describe how you felt (using 2 words) after performing it: _____ & _____

List any challenges you had during the exercise:

_____

_____

Describe two positive and memorable moments, thoughts, or feelings you experienced during the exercise:

_____

_____

_____

Hold the Vision. Trust the Process. Commit to Today.

Today's Date: _____

Learn My Language: What is my language telling me today?

_____

_____

_____

_____

Review My Direction:

Goal #1: _____

What are my reflections about this goal?

_____

_____

_____

_____

Goal #2: _____

What are my reflections about this goal?

_____

_____

_____

_____

Goal #3: _____

What are my reflections about this goal?

_____

_____

_____

_____

Count My Wins:

What did I do today that helped move me closer to achieving my goals? (List everything you can think of.)

_____

_____

_____

_____

_____

_____

_____

_____

My One Thing: Pick one win from above and isolate that as your greatest step towards success.

_____

Imagine Your Outcome.

What time of day did you perform this exercise? _____

Describe how you felt (using 2 words) prior to performing it: _____ & _____

Describe how you felt (using 2 words) after performing it: _____ & _____

List any challenges you had during the exercise:

_____

_____

Describe two positive and memorable moments, thoughts, or feelings you experienced during the exercise:

_____

_____

_____

Hold the Vision. Trust the Process. Commit to Today.

Today's Date: _____

Learn My Language: What is my language telling me today?

_____

_____

_____

_____

Review My Direction:

Goal #1: _____

What are my reflections about this goal?

_____

_____

_____

_____

Goal #2: _____

What are my reflections about this goal?

_____

_____

_____

_____

Goal #3: _____

What are my reflections about this goal?

_____

_____

_____

_____

Count My Wins:

What did I do today that helped move me closer to achieving my goals? (List everything you can think of.)

_____

_____

_____

_____

_____

_____

_____

_____

My One Thing: Pick one win from above and isolate that as your greatest step towards success.

_____

Imagine Your Outcome.

What time of day did you perform this exercise? _____

Describe how you felt (using 2 words) prior to performing it: _____ & _____

Describe how you felt (using 2 words) after performing it: _____ & _____

List any challenges you had during the exercise:

_____

_____

_____

Describe two positive and memorable moments, thoughts, or feelings you experienced during the exercise:

_____

_____

_____

Hold the Vision. Trust the Process. Commit to Today.

Today's Date: _____

Learn My Language: What is my language telling me today?

_____

_____

_____

_____

Review My Direction:

Goal #1: _____

What are my reflections about this goal?

_____

_____

_____

_____

Goal #2: _____

What are my reflections about this goal?

_____

_____

_____

_____

Goal #3: _____

What are my reflections about this goal?

_____

_____

_____

_____

Count My Wins:

What did I do today that helped move me closer to achieving my goals? (List everything you can think of.)

_____

_____

_____

_____

_____

_____

_____

_____

My One Thing: Pick one win from above and isolate that as your greatest step towards success.

_____

Imagine Your Outcome.

What time of day did you perform this exercise? _____

Describe how you felt (using 2 words) prior to performing it: _____ & _____

Describe how you felt (using 2 words) after performing it: _____ & _____

List any challenges you had during the exercise:

_____

_____

_____

Describe two positive and memorable moments, thoughts, or feelings you experienced during the exercise:

_____

_____

_____

Hold the Vision. Trust the Process. Commit to Today.

Today's Date: _____

Learn My Language: What is my language telling me today?

_____

_____

_____

_____

Review My Direction:

Goal #1: _____

What are my reflections about this goal?

_____

_____

_____

_____

Goal #2: _____

What are my reflections about this goal?

_____

_____

_____

_____

Goal #3: _____

What are my reflections about this goal?

_____

_____

_____

_____

Count My Wins:

What did I do today that helped move me closer to achieving my goals? (List everything you can think of.)

_____

_____

_____

_____

_____

_____

_____

_____

My One Thing: Pick one win from above and isolate that as your greatest step towards success.

_____

Imagine Your Outcome.

What time of day did you perform this exercise? _____

Describe how you felt (using 2 words) prior to performing it: _____ & _____

Describe how you felt (using 2 words) after performing it: _____ & _____

List any challenges you had during the exercise:

_____

_____

_____

Describe two positive and memorable moments, thoughts, or feelings you experienced during the exercise:

_____

_____

_____

Hold the Vision. Trust the Process. Commit to Today.

BRIAN & CARRIE
LET'S ELIMINATE YOUR LIMITS
WWW.BRIANANDCARRIE.LIVE

Today's Date: _____

Learn My Language: What is my language telling me today?

_____

_____

_____

_____

Review My Direction:

Goal #1: _____

What are my reflections about this goal?

_____

_____

_____

_____

Goal #2: _____

What are my reflections about this goal?

_____

_____

_____

_____

Goal #3: _____

What are my reflections about this goal?

_____

_____

_____

_____

Count My Wins:

What did I do today that helped move me closer to achieving my goals? (List everything you can think of.)

_____

_____

_____

_____

_____

_____

_____

_____

My One Thing: Pick one win from above and isolate that as your greatest step towards success.

_____

Imagine Your Outcome.

What time of day did you perform this exercise? _____

Describe how you felt (using 2 words) prior to performing it: _____ & _____

Describe how you felt (using 2 words) after performing it: _____ & _____

List any challenges you had during the exercise:

_____

_____

_____

Describe two positive and memorable moments, thoughts, or feelings you experienced during the exercise:

_____

_____

_____

Hold the Vision. Trust the Process. Commit to Today.

BRIAN & CARRIE
LET'S ELIMINATE YOUR LIMITS
WWW.BRIANANDCARRIE.LIVE

Today's Date: _____

Learn My Language: What is my language telling me today?

_____

_____

_____

_____

Review My Direction:

Goal #1: _____

What are my reflections about this goal?

_____

_____

_____

_____

Goal #2: _____

What are my reflections about this goal?

_____

_____

_____

_____

Goal #3: _____

What are my reflections about this goal?

_____

_____

_____

_____

Count My Wins:

What did I do today that helped move me closer to achieving my goals? (List everything you can think of.)

_____

_____

_____

_____

_____

_____

_____

_____

My One Thing: Pick one win from above and isolate that as your greatest step towards success.

_____

Imagine Your Outcome.

What time of day did you perform this exercise? _____

Describe how you felt (using 2 words) prior to performing it: _____ & _____

Describe how you felt (using 2 words) after performing it: _____ & _____

List any challenges you had during the exercise:

_____

_____

_____

Describe two positive and memorable moments, thoughts, or feelings you experienced during the exercise:

_____

_____

_____

Hold the Vision. Trust the Process. Commit to Today.

Today's Date: _____

Learn My Language: What is my language telling me today?

_____

_____

_____

_____

Review My Direction:

Goal #1: _____

What are my reflections about this goal?

_____

_____

_____

_____

Goal #2: _____

What are my reflections about this goal?

_____

_____

_____

_____

Goal #3: _____

What are my reflections about this goal?

_____

_____

_____

_____

Count My Wins:

What did I do today that helped move me closer to achieving my goals? (List everything you can think of.)

_____

_____

_____

_____

_____

_____

_____

_____

My One Thing: Pick one win from above and isolate that as your greatest step towards success.

_____

Imagine Your Outcome.

What time of day did you perform this exercise? _____

Describe how you felt (using 2 words) prior to performing it: _____ & _____

Describe how you felt (using 2 words) after performing it: _____ & _____

List any challenges you had during the exercise:

_____

_____

_____

Describe two positive and memorable moments, thoughts, or feelings you experienced during the exercise:

_____

_____

_____

Hold the Vision. Trust the Process. Commit to Today.

Today's Date: _____

Learn My Language: What is my language telling me today?

_____

_____

_____

_____

Review My Direction:

Goal #1: _____

What are my reflections about this goal?

_____

_____

_____

_____

Goal #2: _____

What are my reflections about this goal?

_____

_____

_____

_____

Goal #3: _____

What are my reflections about this goal?

_____

_____

_____

_____

Count My Wins:

What did I do today that helped move me closer to achieving my goals? (List everything you can think of.)

_____

_____

_____

_____

_____

_____

_____

_____

My One Thing: Pick one win from above and isolate that as your greatest step towards success.

_____

Imagine Your Outcome.

What time of day did you perform this exercise? _____

Describe how you felt (using 2 words) prior to performing it: _____ & _____

Describe how you felt (using 2 words) after performing it: _____ & _____

List any challenges you had during the exercise:

_____

_____

_____

Describe two positive and memorable moments, thoughts, or feelings you experienced during the exercise:

_____

_____

_____

Hold the Vision. Trust the Process. Commit to Today.

Today's Date: _____

Learn My Language: What is my language telling me today?

_____

_____

_____

_____

Review My Direction:

Goal #1: _____

What are my reflections about this goal?

_____

_____

_____

_____

Goal #2: _____

What are my reflections about this goal?

_____

_____

_____

_____

Goal #3: _____

What are my reflections about this goal?

_____

_____

_____

_____

Count My Wins:

What did I do today that helped move me closer to achieving my goals? (List everything you can think of.)

_____

_____

_____

_____

_____

_____

_____

_____

My One Thing: Pick one win from above and isolate that as your greatest step towards success.

_____

Imagine Your Outcome.

What time of day did you perform this exercise? _____

Describe how you felt (using 2 words) prior to performing it: _____ & _____

Describe how you felt (using 2 words) after performing it: _____ & _____

List any challenges you had during the exercise:

_____

_____

_____

Describe two positive and memorable moments, thoughts, or feelings you experienced during the exercise:

_____

_____

_____

Hold the Vision. Trust the Process. Commit to Today.

Today's Date: _____

Learn My Language: What is my language telling me today?

_____

_____

_____

_____

Review My Direction:

Goal #1: _____

What are my reflections about this goal?

_____

_____

_____

_____

Goal #2: _____

What are my reflections about this goal?

_____

_____

_____

_____

Goal #3: _____

What are my reflections about this goal?

_____

_____

_____

_____

Count My Wins:

What did I do today that helped move me closer to achieving my goals? (List everything you can think of.)

_____

_____

_____

_____

_____

_____

_____

_____

My One Thing: Pick one win from above and isolate that as your greatest step towards success.

_____

Imagine Your Outcome.

What time of day did you perform this exercise? _____

Describe how you felt (using 2 words) prior to performing it: _____ & _____

Describe how you felt (using 2 words) after performing it: _____ & _____

List any challenges you had during the exercise:

_____

_____

_____

Describe two positive and memorable moments, thoughts, or feelings you experienced during the exercise:

_____

_____

_____

Hold the Vision. Trust the Process. Commit to Today.

Today's Date: _____

Learn My Language: What is my language telling me today?

_____

_____

_____

_____

Review My Direction:

Goal #1: _____

What are my reflections about this goal?

_____

_____

_____

_____

Goal #2: _____

What are my reflections about this goal?

_____

_____

_____

_____

Goal #3: _____

What are my reflections about this goal?

_____

_____

_____

_____

Count My Wins:

What did I do today that helped move me closer to achieving my goals? (List everything you can think of.)

_____

_____

_____

_____

_____

_____

_____

_____

My One Thing: Pick one win from above and isolate that as your greatest step towards success.

_____

Imagine Your Outcome.

What time of day did you perform this exercise? _____

Describe how you felt (using 2 words) prior to performing it: _____ & _____

Describe how you felt (using 2 words) after performing it: _____ & _____

List any challenges you had during the exercise:

_____

_____

_____

Describe two positive and memorable moments, thoughts, or feelings you experienced during the exercise:

_____

_____

_____

Hold the Vision. Trust the Process. Commit to Today.

Today's Date: _____

Learn My Language: What is my language telling me today?

_____

_____

_____

_____

Review My Direction:

Goal #1: _____

What are my reflections about this goal?

_____

_____

_____

_____

Goal #2: _____

What are my reflections about this goal?

_____

_____

_____

_____

Goal #3: _____

What are my reflections about this goal?

_____

_____

_____

_____

Count My Wins:

What did I do today that helped move me closer to achieving my goals? (List everything you can think of.)

_____

_____

_____

_____

_____

_____

_____

My One Thing: Pick one win from above and isolate that as your greatest step towards success.

_____

Imagine Your Outcome.

What time of day did you perform this exercise? _____

Describe how you felt (using 2 words) prior to performing it: _____ & _____

Describe how you felt (using 2 words) after performing it: _____ & _____

List any challenges you had during the exercise:

_____

_____

Describe two positive and memorable moments, thoughts, or feelings you experienced during the exercise:

_____

_____

_____

Hold the Vision. Trust the Process. Commit to Today.

Today's Date: _____

Learn My Language: What is my language telling me today?

_____

_____

_____

_____

Review My Direction:

Goal #1: _____

What are my reflections about this goal?

_____

_____

_____

_____

Goal #2: _____

What are my reflections about this goal?

_____

_____

_____

_____

Goal #3: _____

What are my reflections about this goal?

_____

_____

_____

_____

Count My Wins:

What did I do today that helped move me closer to achieving my goals? (List everything you can think of.)

_____

_____

_____

_____

_____

_____

_____

_____

My One Thing: Pick one win from above and isolate that as your greatest step towards success.

_____

Imagine Your Outcome.

What time of day did you perform this exercise? _____

Describe how you felt (using 2 words) prior to performing it: _____ & _____

Describe how you felt (using 2 words) after performing it: _____ & _____

List any challenges you had during the exercise:

_____

_____

_____

Describe two positive and memorable moments, thoughts, or feelings you experienced during the exercise:

_____

_____

_____

Hold the Vision. Trust the Process. Commit to Today.

Today's Date: _____

Learn My Language: What is my language telling me today?

_____

_____

_____

_____

Review My Direction:

Goal #1: _____

What are my reflections about this goal?

_____

_____

_____

_____

Goal #2: _____

What are my reflections about this goal?

_____

_____

_____

_____

Goal #3: _____

What are my reflections about this goal?

_____

_____

_____

_____

Count My Wins:

What did I do today that helped move me closer to achieving my goals? (List everything you can think of.)

_____

_____

_____

_____

_____

_____

_____

_____

My One Thing: Pick one win from above and isolate that as your greatest step towards success.

_____

Imagine Your Outcome.

What time of day did you perform this exercise? _____

Describe how you felt (using 2 words) prior to performing it: _____ & _____

Describe how you felt (using 2 words) after performing it: _____ & _____

List any challenges you had during the exercise:

_____

_____

_____

Describe two positive and memorable moments, thoughts, or feelings you experienced during the exercise:

_____

_____

_____

Hold the Vision. Trust the Process. Commit to Today.

Today's Date: _____

Learn My Language: What is my language telling me today?

_____

_____

_____

_____

Review My Direction:

Goal #1: _____

What are my reflections about this goal?

_____

_____

_____

_____

Goal #2: _____

What are my reflections about this goal?

_____

_____

_____

_____

Goal #3: _____

What are my reflections about this goal?

_____

_____

_____

_____

Count My Wins:

What did I do today that helped move me closer to achieving my goals? (List everything you can think of.)

_____

_____

_____

_____

_____

_____

_____

_____

My One Thing: Pick one win from above and isolate that as your greatest step towards success.

_____

Imagine Your Outcome.

What time of day did you perform this exercise? _____

Describe how you felt (using 2 words) prior to performing it: _____ & _____

Describe how you felt (using 2 words) after performing it: _____ & _____

List any challenges you had during the exercise:

_____

_____

_____

Describe two positive and memorable moments, thoughts, or feelings you experienced during the exercise:

_____

_____

_____

Hold the Vision. Trust the Process. Commit to Today.

Today's Date: _____

Learn My Language: What is my language telling me today?

_____

_____

_____

_____

Review My Direction:

Goal #1: _____

What are my reflections about this goal?

_____

_____

_____

_____

Goal #2: _____

What are my reflections about this goal?

_____

_____

_____

_____

Goal #3: _____

What are my reflections about this goal?

_____

_____

_____

_____

Count My Wins:

What did I do today that helped move me closer to achieving my goals? (List everything you can think of.)

_____

_____

_____

_____

_____

_____

_____

_____

My One Thing: Pick one win from above and isolate that as your greatest step towards success.

_____

Imagine Your Outcome.

What time of day did you perform this exercise? _____

Describe how you felt (using 2 words) prior to performing it: _____ & _____

Describe how you felt (using 2 words) after performing it: _____ & _____

List any challenges you had during the exercise:

_____

_____

_____

Describe two positive and memorable moments, thoughts, or feelings you experienced during the exercise:

_____

_____

_____

Hold the Vision. Trust the Process. Commit to Today.

Today's Date: _____

Learn My Language: What is my language telling me today?

_____

_____

_____

_____

Review My Direction:

Goal #1: _____

What are my reflections about this goal?

_____

_____

_____

_____

Goal #2: _____

What are my reflections about this goal?

_____

_____

_____

_____

Goal #3: _____

What are my reflections about this goal?

_____

_____

_____

_____

Count My Wins:

What did I do today that helped move me closer to achieving my goals? (List everything you can think of.)

_____

_____

_____

_____

_____

_____

_____

_____

My One Thing: Pick one win from above and isolate that as your greatest step towards success.

_____

Imagine Your Outcome.

What time of day did you perform this exercise? _____

Describe how you felt (using 2 words) prior to performing it: _____ & _____

Describe how you felt (using 2 words) after performing it: _____ & _____

List any challenges you had during the exercise:

_____

_____

_____

Describe two positive and memorable moments, thoughts, or feelings you experienced during the exercise:

_____

_____

_____

Hold the Vision. Trust the Process. Commit to Today.

Today's Date: _____

Learn My Language: What is my language telling me today?

_____

_____

_____

_____

Review My Direction:

Goal #1: _____

What are my reflections about this goal?

_____

_____

_____

_____

Goal #2: _____

What are my reflections about this goal?

_____

_____

_____

_____

Goal #3: _____

What are my reflections about this goal?

_____

_____

_____

_____

Count My Wins:

What did I do today that helped move me closer to achieving my goals? (List everything you can think of.)

_____

_____

_____

_____

_____

_____

_____

My One Thing: Pick one win from above and isolate that as your greatest step towards success.

_____

Imagine Your Outcome.

What time of day did you perform this exercise? _____

Describe how you felt (using 2 words) prior to performing it: _____ & _____

Describe how you felt (using 2 words) after performing it: _____ & _____

List any challenges you had during the exercise:

_____

_____

_____

Describe two positive and memorable moments, thoughts, or feelings you experienced during the exercise:

_____

_____

_____

Hold the Vision. Trust the Process. Commit to Today.

BRIAN & CARRIE
LET'S ELIMINATE YOUR LIMITS
WWW.BRIANANDCARRIE.LIVE

Today's Date: _____

Learn My Language: What is my language telling me today?

_____

_____

_____

_____

Review My Direction:

Goal #1: _____

What are my reflections about this goal?

_____

_____

_____

_____

Goal #2: _____

What are my reflections about this goal?

_____

_____

_____

_____

Goal #3: _____

What are my reflections about this goal?

_____

_____

_____

_____

Count My Wins:

What did I do today that helped move me closer to achieving my goals? (List everything you can think of.)

_____

_____

_____

_____

_____

_____

_____

_____

My One Thing: Pick one win from above and isolate that as your greatest step towards success.

_____

Imagine Your Outcome.

What time of day did you perform this exercise? _____

Describe how you felt (using 2 words) prior to performing it: _____ & _____

Describe how you felt (using 2 words) after performing it: _____ & _____

List any challenges you had during the exercise:

_____

_____

_____

Describe two positive and memorable moments, thoughts, or feelings you experienced during the exercise:

_____

_____

_____

Hold the Vision. Trust the Process. Commit to Today.

Today's Date: _____

Learn My Language: What is my language telling me today?

_____

_____

_____

_____

Review My Direction:

Goal #1: _____

What are my reflections about this goal?

_____

_____

_____

_____

Goal #2: _____

What are my reflections about this goal?

_____

_____

_____

_____

Goal #3: _____

What are my reflections about this goal?

_____

_____

_____

_____

Count My Wins:

What did I do today that helped move me closer to achieving my goals? (List everything you can think of.)

_____

_____

_____

_____

_____

_____

_____

_____

My One Thing: Pick one win from above and isolate that as your greatest step towards success.

_____

Imagine Your Outcome.

What time of day did you perform this exercise? _____

Describe how you felt (using 2 words) prior to performing it: _____ & _____

Describe how you felt (using 2 words) after performing it: _____ & _____

List any challenges you had during the exercise:

_____

_____

Describe two positive and memorable moments, thoughts, or feelings you experienced during the exercise:

_____

_____

_____

Hold the Vision. Trust the Process. Commit to Today.

Today's Date: _____

Learn My Language: What is my language telling me today?

_____

_____

_____

_____

Review My Direction:

Goal #1: _____

What are my reflections about this goal?

_____

_____

_____

_____

Goal #2: _____

What are my reflections about this goal?

_____

_____

_____

_____

Goal #3: _____

What are my reflections about this goal?

_____

_____

_____

_____

Count My Wins:

What did I do today that helped move me closer to achieving my goals? (List everything you can think of.)

_____

_____

_____

_____

_____

_____

_____

My One Thing: Pick one win from above and isolate that as your greatest step towards success.

_____

Imagine Your Outcome.

What time of day did you perform this exercise? _____

Describe how you felt (using 2 words) prior to performing it: _____ & _____

Describe how you felt (using 2 words) after performing it: _____ & _____

List any challenges you had during the exercise:

_____

_____

Describe two positive and memorable moments, thoughts, or feelings you experienced during the exercise:

_____

_____

_____

Hold the Vision. Trust the Process. Commit to Today.

Today's Date: _____

Learn My Language: What is my language telling me today?

_____

_____

_____

_____

Review My Direction:

Goal #1: _____

What are my reflections about this goal?

_____

_____

_____

_____

Goal #2: _____

What are my reflections about this goal?

_____

_____

_____

_____

Goal #3: _____

What are my reflections about this goal?

_____

_____

_____

_____

Count My Wins:

What did I do today that helped move me closer to achieving my goals? (List everything you can think of.)

_____

_____

_____

_____

_____

_____

_____

My One Thing: Pick one win from above and isolate that as your greatest step towards success.

_____

Imagine Your Outcome.

What time of day did you perform this exercise? _____

Describe how you felt (using 2 words) prior to performing it: _____ & _____

Describe how you felt (using 2 words) after performing it: _____ & _____

List any challenges you had during the exercise:

_____

_____

_____

Describe two positive and memorable moments, thoughts, or feelings you experienced during the exercise:

_____

_____

_____

Hold the Vision. Trust the Process. Commit to Today.

Today's Date: _____

Learn My Language: What is my language telling me today?

_____

_____

_____

_____

Review My Direction:

Goal #1: _____

What are my reflections about this goal?

_____

_____

_____

_____

Goal #2: _____

What are my reflections about this goal?

_____

_____

_____

_____

Goal #3: _____

What are my reflections about this goal?

_____

_____

_____

_____

Count My Wins:

What did I do today that helped move me closer to achieving my goals? (List everything you can think of.)

_____

_____

_____

_____

_____

_____

_____

_____

My One Thing: Pick one win from above and isolate that as your greatest step towards success.

_____

Imagine Your Outcome.

What time of day did you perform this exercise? _____

Describe how you felt (using 2 words) prior to performing it: _____ & _____

Describe how you felt (using 2 words) after performing it: _____ & _____

List any challenges you had during the exercise:

_____

_____

_____

Describe two positive and memorable moments, thoughts, or feelings you experienced during the exercise:

_____

_____

_____

Hold the Vision. Trust the Process. Commit to Today.

Today's Date: _____

Learn My Language: What is my language telling me today?

_____

_____

_____

_____

Review My Direction:

Goal #1: _____

What are my reflections about this goal?

_____

_____

_____

_____

Goal #2: _____

What are my reflections about this goal?

_____

_____

_____

_____

Goal #3: _____

What are my reflections about this goal?

_____

_____

_____

_____

Count My Wins:

What did I do today that helped move me closer to achieving my goals? (List everything you can think of.)

_____

_____

_____

_____

_____

_____

_____

_____

My One Thing: Pick one win from above and isolate that as your greatest step towards success.

_____

Imagine Your Outcome.

What time of day did you perform this exercise? _____

Describe how you felt (using 2 words) prior to performing it: _____ & _____

Describe how you felt (using 2 words) after performing it: _____ & _____

List any challenges you had during the exercise:

_____

_____

Describe two positive and memorable moments, thoughts, or feelings you experienced during the exercise:

_____

_____

_____

Hold the Vision. Trust the Process. Commit to Today.

Today's Date: _____

Learn My Language: What is my language telling me today?

_____

_____

_____

_____

Review My Direction:

Goal #1: _____

What are my reflections about this goal?

_____

_____

_____

_____

Goal #2: _____

What are my reflections about this goal?

_____

_____

_____

_____

Goal #3: _____

What are my reflections about this goal?

_____

_____

_____

_____

Count My Wins:

What did I do today that helped move me closer to achieving my goals? (List everything you can think of.)

_____

_____

_____

_____

_____

_____

_____

_____

My One Thing: Pick one win from above and isolate that as your greatest step towards success.

_____

Imagine Your Outcome.

What time of day did you perform this exercise? _____

Describe how you felt (using 2 words) prior to performing it: _____ & _____

Describe how you felt (using 2 words) after performing it: _____ & _____

List any challenges you had during the exercise:

_____

_____

_____

Describe two positive and memorable moments, thoughts, or feelings you experienced during the exercise:

_____

_____

_____

Hold the Vision. Trust the Process. Commit to Today.

Today's Date: _____

Learn My Language: What is my language telling me today?

_____

_____

_____

_____

Review My Direction:

Goal #1: _____

What are my reflections about this goal?

_____

_____

_____

_____

Goal #2: _____

What are my reflections about this goal?

_____

_____

_____

_____

Goal #3: _____

What are my reflections about this goal?

_____

_____

_____

_____

Count My Wins:

What did I do today that helped move me closer to achieving my goals? (List everything you can think of.)

_____

_____

_____

_____

_____

_____

_____

_____

My One Thing: Pick one win from above and isolate that as your greatest step towards success.

_____

Imagine Your Outcome.

What time of day did you perform this exercise? _____

Describe how you felt (using 2 words) prior to performing it: _____ & _____

Describe how you felt (using 2 words) after performing it: _____ & _____

List any challenges you had during the exercise:

_____

_____

_____

Describe two positive and memorable moments, thoughts, or feelings you experienced during the exercise:

_____

_____

_____

Hold the Vision. Trust the Process. Commit to Today.

Today's Date: _____

Learn My Language: What is my language telling me today?

_____

_____

_____

_____

Review My Direction:

Goal #1: _____

What are my reflections about this goal?

_____

_____

_____

_____

Goal #2: _____

What are my reflections about this goal?

_____

_____

_____

_____

Goal #3: _____

What are my reflections about this goal?

_____

_____

_____

_____

Count My Wins:

What did I do today that helped move me closer to achieving my goals? (List everything you can think of.)

_____

_____

_____

_____

_____

_____

_____

My One Thing: Pick one win from above and isolate that as your greatest step towards success.

_____

Imagine Your Outcome.

What time of day did you perform this exercise? _____

Describe how you felt (using 2 words) prior to performing it: _____ & _____

Describe how you felt (using 2 words) after performing it: _____ & _____

List any challenges you had during the exercise:

_____

_____

_____

Describe two positive and memorable moments, thoughts, or feelings you experienced during the exercise:

_____

_____

_____

Hold the Vision. Trust the Process. Commit to Today.

Today's Date: _____

Learn My Language: What is my language telling me today?

_____

_____

_____

_____

Review My Direction:

Goal #1: _____

What are my reflections about this goal?

_____

_____

_____

_____

Goal #2: _____

What are my reflections about this goal?

_____

_____

_____

_____

Goal #3: _____

What are my reflections about this goal?

_____

_____

_____

_____

Count My Wins:

What did I do today that helped move me closer to achieving my goals? (List everything you can think of.)

_____

_____

_____

_____

_____

_____

_____

_____

My One Thing: Pick one win from above and isolate that as your greatest step towards success.

_____

Imagine Your Outcome.

What time of day did you perform this exercise? _____

Describe how you felt (using 2 words) prior to performing it: _____ & _____

Describe how you felt (using 2 words) after performing it: _____ & _____

List any challenges you had during the exercise:

_____

_____

_____

Describe two positive and memorable moments, thoughts, or feelings you experienced during the exercise:

_____

_____

_____

Hold the Vision. Trust the Process. Commit to Today.

Today's Date: _____

Learn My Language: What is my language telling me today?

_____

_____

_____

_____

Review My Direction:

Goal #1: _____

What are my reflections about this goal?

_____

_____

_____

_____

Goal #2: _____

What are my reflections about this goal?

_____

_____

_____

_____

Goal #3: _____

What are my reflections about this goal?

_____

_____

_____

_____

Count My Wins:

What did I do today that helped move me closer to achieving my goals? (List everything you can think of.)

_____

_____

_____

_____

_____

_____

_____

_____

My One Thing: Pick one win from above and isolate that as your greatest step towards success.

_____

Imagine Your Outcome.

What time of day did you perform this exercise? _____

Describe how you felt (using 2 words) prior to performing it: _____ & _____

Describe how you felt (using 2 words) after performing it: _____ & _____

List any challenges you had during the exercise:

_____

_____

_____

Describe two positive and memorable moments, thoughts, or feelings you experienced during the exercise:

_____

_____

_____

Hold the Vision. Trust the Process. Commit to Today.

Today's Date: _____

Learn My Language: What is my language telling me today?

_____

_____

_____

_____

Review My Direction:

Goal #1: _____

What are my reflections about this goal?

_____

_____

_____

_____

Goal #2: _____

What are my reflections about this goal?

_____

_____

_____

_____

Goal #3: _____

What are my reflections about this goal?

_____

_____

_____

_____

Count My Wins:

What did I do today that helped move me closer to achieving my goals? (List everything you can think of.)

_____

_____

_____

_____

_____

_____

_____

_____

My One Thing: Pick one win from above and isolate that as your greatest step towards success.

_____

Imagine Your Outcome.

What time of day did you perform this exercise? _____

Describe how you felt (using 2 words) prior to performing it: _____ & _____

Describe how you felt (using 2 words) after performing it: _____ & _____

List any challenges you had during the exercise:

_____

_____

_____

Describe two positive and memorable moments, thoughts, or feelings you experienced during the exercise:

_____

_____

_____

Hold the Vision. Trust the Process. Commit to Today.

Today's Date: _____

Learn My Language: What is my language telling me today?

_____

_____

_____

_____

Review My Direction:

Goal #1: _____

What are my reflections about this goal?

_____

_____

_____

_____

Goal #2: _____

What are my reflections about this goal?

_____

_____

_____

_____

Goal #3: _____

What are my reflections about this goal?

_____

_____

_____

_____

Count My Wins:

What did I do today that helped move me closer to achieving my goals? (List everything you can think of.)

_____

_____

_____

_____

_____

_____

_____

_____

My One Thing: Pick one win from above and isolate that as your greatest step towards success.

_____

Imagine Your Outcome.

What time of day did you perform this exercise? _____

Describe how you felt (using 2 words) prior to performing it: _____ & _____

Describe how you felt (using 2 words) after performing it: _____ & _____

List any challenges you had during the exercise:

_____

_____

Describe two positive and memorable moments, thoughts, or feelings you experienced during the exercise:

_____

_____

_____

Hold the Vision. Trust the Process. Commit to Today.

Today's Date: _____

Learn My Language: What is my language telling me today?

_____

_____

_____

_____

Review My Direction:

Goal #1: _____

What are my reflections about this goal?

_____

_____

_____

_____

Goal #2: _____

What are my reflections about this goal?

_____

_____

_____

_____

Goal #3: _____

What are my reflections about this goal?

_____

_____

_____

_____

Count My Wins:

What did I do today that helped move me closer to achieving my goals? (List everything you can think of.)

_____

_____

_____

_____

_____

_____

_____

_____

My One Thing: Pick one win from above and isolate that as your greatest step towards success.

_____

Imagine Your Outcome.

What time of day did you perform this exercise? _____

Describe how you felt (using 2 words) prior to performing it: _____ & _____

Describe how you felt (using 2 words) after performing it: _____ & _____

List any challenges you had during the exercise:

_____

_____

Describe two positive and memorable moments, thoughts, or feelings you experienced during the exercise:

_____

_____

_____

Hold the Vision. Trust the Process. Commit to Today.

Today's Date: _____

Learn My Language: What is my language telling me today?

_____

_____

_____

_____

Review My Direction:

Goal #1: _____

What are my reflections about this goal?

_____

_____

_____

_____

Goal #2: _____

What are my reflections about this goal?

_____

_____

_____

_____

Goal #3: _____

What are my reflections about this goal?

_____

_____

_____

_____

Count My Wins:

What did I do today that helped move me closer to achieving my goals? (List everything you can think of.)

_____

_____

_____

_____

_____

_____

_____

My One Thing: Pick one win from above and isolate that as your greatest step towards success.

_____

Imagine Your Outcome.

What time of day did you perform this exercise? _____

Describe how you felt (using 2 words) prior to performing it: _____ & _____

Describe how you felt (using 2 words) after performing it: _____ & _____

List any challenges you had during the exercise:

_____

_____

Describe two positive and memorable moments, thoughts, or feelings you experienced during the exercise:

_____

_____

_____

Hold the Vision. Trust the Process. Commit to Today.

Today's Date: _____

Learn My Language: What is my language telling me today?

_____

_____

_____

_____

Review My Direction:

Goal #1: _____

What are my reflections about this goal?

_____

_____

_____

_____

Goal #2: _____

What are my reflections about this goal?

_____

_____

_____

_____

Goal #3: _____

What are my reflections about this goal?

_____

_____

_____

_____

Count My Wins:

What did I do today that helped move me closer to achieving my goals? (List everything you can think of.)

_____

_____

_____

_____

_____

_____

_____

_____

My One Thing: Pick one win from above and isolate that as your greatest step towards success.

_____

Imagine Your Outcome.

What time of day did you perform this exercise? _____

Describe how you felt (using 2 words) prior to performing it: _____ & _____

Describe how you felt (using 2 words) after performing it: _____ & _____

List any challenges you had during the exercise:

_____

_____

_____

Describe two positive and memorable moments, thoughts, or feelings you experienced during the exercise:

_____

_____

_____

Hold the Vision. Trust the Process. Commit to Today.

Overcome your obstacles with ease & achieve exactly what you want in life.

❧❧❧

ENLIST NO OPPONENT.

That's the best possible advice we could give you.

But it's advice you seldom hear anywhere else.

Your unconscious is the most powerful and limitless instrument known to humankind.

It builds in your life what you ask of it in your dreams.

And it does so without questions, objections, or knowledge of what is real versus imagined.

So no matter your goal, don't define it as something you have to "fight" for.

Don't determine it to be "hard."

Don't refer to it as "overcoming obstacles."

And don't consider it something that needs "willpower."

That's creating an "opponent" for no reason.

It takes what can be achieved simply and adds the complexity of "challenge."

There really is nothing in your way.

Nothing, but you.

Every morning, we chart our path for the next five years.

The conversation lasts 20 minutes.

The image is clear, the journey simple, and the outcome guaranteed.

What amounts to something most would consider "unlikely," "pie in the sky," and "lofty," we choose to define as "effortless."

Which is precisely why it will work.

No "fight."

No "hard."

No "challenge."

No "willpower."

And no "opponent."

Don't get caught up in the haze of those motivational battle cries.

Don't accept the negative self-talk that calls you inferior, unable, or not worthy.

Because the hardest thing to understand...

...is just how simple it all really is.

৶৶৶

Which is why we'd like to talk to you about our "Mentor Method."

It's a method that, once introduced into your life, won't just be the reason you finally achieve the goals you set. It will also show you how to find and live your life's purpose.

So much so, in fact, that you'll actually be able to learn how to set even bigger goals and truly live the life you've always wanted.

This is the highest impact and biggest game-changing advancement in goal-setting success ever created.

Because this simple method has been field-tested and proven effective for men and women all over the world.

Including Olympic and professional athletes to improve focus, concentration, and confidence.

Entrepreneurs taking their businesses to the next level of income and impact by enhancing their time management and creativity.

And exercise enthusiasts who finally lose weight and easily keep it off.

All you need to do is text the word "BRIANandCARRIE" to 707-240-4233.

That's it.

Do that, and we'll share with you – directly – the insider information that has transformed lives around the world.

The simple method for finding & living your life's purpose.

❧❧❧

That's what our "Mentor Model" is all about.

And this is why...

"Until you make the unconscious conscious, it will direct your life and you will call it fate."

That quote from Carl Jung is a game-changer.

And a life-changer, if you just pause to give it some reflection.

Whether you know us personally or "know" us through Facebook, you wouldn't have recognized the people we were, had we been friends ten years ago.

We were angry.

Frustrated.

Jealous.

Jaded.

But mostly, so terribly sad.

Sad because we had tried absolutely everything you were supposed to try.

We followed the goal-setting experts.

Listened to the success gurus.

And did the work that the "hustle" authorities claim is required.

None of it worked for us.

Our days were spent in this frenzy of commotion. Charting our goals, reading every book we could get our hands on, and working our collective asses off to make it all come together.

In contrast, our nights were spent in a pit of grief.

In disbelief that we would ever achieve our goals and absolutely exhausted from another 24-hour cycle of trying to make it happen.

We started believing we were broken.

That, while our friends and colleagues were crushing it and on the cusp of even greater heights, we were bound for mediocrity.

Destined to be inferior.

That somehow we lacked the smarts, the ability, or the savvy to achieve what we wanted.

That was our fate.

Until we started making our unconscious conscious.

ക&ക&ക

The game-changer and life-changer for us had nothing to do with setting more goals, reading more books or hustling harder...
...It had to do with learning to understand what Mindset is, how it works and how ours was keeping us stuck.

ക&ക&ക

Success – we came to realize – wasn't about working to become successful so much as releasing yourself from the reasons you're not.

We both had a "story" in our unconscious.

And, without realizing it, that "story" played on repeat. All day. Every day.

It was the cause and source of something both you and we know very well:

Self-sabotage.

We knew what to do and, in most cases, even how to do it.

But there was something preventing us from actually getting it done.

We live in such a testosterone-heavy culture that is forever telling us to just "kick the door down," "get after it," "be relentless," and "kill it."

That stuff never worked for us. And I'll bet it doesn't work for you sustainably, either.

The "gentle way" is too often confused for being less effective or somehow a "wussification" type of path, maybe because it lacks the dramatics of most motivational messages we get bombarded with over and over again.

But it is the only way that creates lasting change and sustainability.

You have an internal dialogue.

An unconscious "story" that is speaking to you at every moment of every day.

95 percent of the time, you pay no attention to it whatsoever.

But it controls your life.

It's what makes the path simple or hard.

What makes the venture successful or not.

What makes you happy and fulfilled or miserable and unsatisfied.

Until you make that "story" conscious and realize that you have the power to change it whenever you want to, it will direct your life.

And you will call it fate.

If you've wanted to:

- ✓ Make more money
- ✓ Grow a successful business
- ✓ Finally make real the dream you've been carrying in your heart
- ✓ Lose the weight and keep it off
- ✓ Increase your self-worth
- ✓ Get that job promotion
- ✓ Stop feeling so stuck and helpless

… But can't.

No matter what you do or how hard you try.

We'd ask you to give this a serious read.

Because there are VERY FEW people in the world who WON'T resonate with what we just wrote above.

Truth is, it's not nearly as difficult, challenging, or "mystic" as the woo-woo people always make it seem and sound.

We're talking about a pretty basic process that is both simple to implement and allows for ever-expanding growth.

Which leads us to the first point you absolutely MUST follow:

SIMPLICITY + CONSISTENCY = SUCCESS

Every single time.

> In business.
> In fitness.
> In relationships.
> In life.

Do simple things.

Do them consistently every day.

The result is both predictable and ironclad.

Truth is...

Maybe you don't need to set goals.

Maybe a vision board is the exact opposite of what you need.

Maybe the positive affirmations you say work against you.

And maybe meditation shouldn't be on your daily menu of to do activities for now.

25 years spent doing practical Mindset work has shown us two things:

> (1) There's isn't "A" way... There's "YOUR" way.

> (2) The very best Mindset practices are the ones that meet you where you are.

Number 2 in particular is something way too many "experts" and "authorities" on the subject miss.

If you're not assessing, you're guessing.

If you don't diagnose, the prescription could be both flawed and dangerous.

No one doubts those two statements when it comes to physical fitness.

Medicine. Even business consulting.

Before we decide on a "solution," we have to understand the "problem."

- ❖ Explicit
- ❖ Inspirit
- ❖ Ambassador
- ❖ Mentor

Those represent the four classifications we've taken years to understand.

People in the Explicit model tend to be very sad and live in various degrees of despair.

Inspirit types react to life events and often seem to be on emotional rollercoaster of highs and lows.

Ambassadors accept the journey of life, are highly aware, and continually evolve.

The Mentor classification represents people who are eager to grow, but can often become impatient when they don't grow at the rate they expect to.

Four completely different types of people.

With four different sets of needs.

Goals are great.

Vision boards can be very powerful.

Positive affirmations: effective.

And meditation: undeniably important.

But that doesn't mean they will all prove positive for everyone.

Ever spent time creating goals but then end up NOT pursuing them within just a few days or weeks?

Ever take hours to build a vision board, only to realize that you've started looking at it with CONTEMPT or ANGER?

Ever find yourself feeling HOPELESS or in DISBELIEF after repeating positive affirmations?

Ever give up on meditation because it causes you more STRAIN and FRUSTRATION than it does anything else?

There is no "one-size-fits-all" for...

> Exercise
> Nutrition
> Medicine
> Relationships
> Financial Investments
> ... or anything else.

Which is why we work under the concept of ONE-SIZE-FITS-ONE.

TRULY tapping into your potential and undoing those unconscious stories that keep you swimming in the seas of over-thinking, procrastination, and self-doubt is always going to be about creating the solution that **you** need.

You cannot EVER out-goal-set an unsuccessful mindset.

So let us show you the way.

YOUR way.

All you need to do is text the word "BRIANandCARRIE" to 707-240-4233.

Let's eliminate your limits… together.

Text us now ("BRIANandCARRIE" to 707-240-4233).

You know it's time.

So do we.

Brian & Carrie

P.S. - Just text the word "BRIANandCARRIE" to 707-240-4233…. Right now!

ళళళ

NOTES

જ્જ્જ

Made in the USA
San Bernardino, CA
19 January 2017